EX LIBRIS

FROM THE LIBRARY OF

*I WAS SHOWING THE AMERICA
I KNEW AND OBSERVED TO OTHERS
WHO MIGHT NOT HAVE NOTICED*

-NORMAN ROCKWELL-

NORMAN ROCKWELL'S AMERICA
...IN
ENGLAND

JUDY GOFFMAN CUTLER
LAURENCE S. CUTLER

NATIONAL MUSEUM OF
AMERICAN ILLUSTRATION
&
DULWICH PICTURE GALLERY

★ ★ ★ ★ ★

DULWICH PICTURE GALLERY
LONDON, ENGLAND

★

NATIONAL MUSEUM OF AMERICAN ILLUSTRATION
NEWPORT, RHODE ISLAND, US

DEDICATION

Norman Percevel Rockwell's sons,
Jarvis, Tommy and Peter Rockwell
for their help over the years

and to our late
NMAI Advisory Board Members
•
J. Carter Brown
Director Emeritus, National Gallery of Art
•
Giulio Cesare Carani
International Art and Antiques Expert
•
Ralph Emerson Carpenter, Jr.
Furniture Historian and Preservationist
•
Chauncey Dewey
World Bank Officer & Preservationist
•
Martin Meyerson
President, University of Pennsylvania
•
US Sen. Claiborne Pell
National Leader *par excellence*
•
and finally to the late, dear
Martin Bressler, Esq.
Art Lawyer *extraordinaire*

Cutler, Judy Goffman
Norman Rockwell's America... in England by Judy Goffman Cutler and Laurence S. Cutler
ISBN 9780-615-41362-4

Text: Copyright © 2010 by Judy Goffman Cutler and Laurence S. Cutler and
National Museum of American Illustration™ Newport, RI, US
www.AmericanIllustration.org

Published images and photographs unless otherwise noted:
Courtesy Archives of National Museum of American Illustration™ Newport, RI, US
www.AmericanIllustration.org
Copyright © 2010 Archives of American Illustrators Gallery™ NYC
www.AmericanIllustrators.com

Saturday Evening Post cover images © *SEPS*: www.curtispublishing.com
Inside Cover Frame: Late 17th Century Spanish Baroque Frame by Julius Lowy Framing and Restoration

Photographs pages: 58, 66, 140, 144, 146, 156, 157, 208, 216: Courtesy Norman Rockwell Museum Archives
Images of Old Master artworks pages: 56, 62, 65, 99: © Trustees of Dulwich Picture Gallery

Front cover:	Detail from Norman Rockwell's *Doughboy and his Admirers*
Endpapers:	Detail from Norman Rockwell's *Bridge Game - The Bid*
Page 5:	Detail from Norman Rockwell's *Threading the Needle*
Frontispiece:	Photograph of Norman Rockwell in his studio, circa 1922
Back Cover:	Detail from Norman Rockwell's *Winchester Stage Coach*

The American Civilization Foundation, Newport, R.I., US - Publisher

CONTENTS

NMAI Founders' Statement

For more than sixty years, Norman Rockwell reflected the currents of American life and its times, from his earliest drawings to patriotic themes and to more socially conscious images in his later years. It has been said that his genius was to capture the essence of what is now considered largely 'a vanished America.' Before the media revolution and an age driven by computers, the public looked forward to and identified with magazine covers-their only means to see images. And Rockwell's covers best captured the emotions of the times.

In fact, from images printed in periodicals and books, many know 'the look' of Norman Rockwell art, but not the art itself. The public still often fails to realize that there was an oil painting behind each printed image. One look at an original Rockwell painting will make apparent the quality and depth of his talent, style, technique, craftsmanship and place as one of the most important American artists.

Rockwell's earliest inspiration came from his father, and indirectly from his grandfather's primitive canvases of bucolic scenes. After dropping out of high school, he enrolled at the Art Students League where he was taught anatomical accuracy and composition. While he followed the nineteenth-century genre painters and consequently painted 'slices of life,' the most popular illustrators of his youth were Maxfield Parrish and J.C. Leyendecker. They were powerful influences on his development as an artist as were the Old Masters and even Picasso. But his admiration for J.C. Leyendecker was so obsessive that he ultimately devoted a chapter of his autobiography, to him.

In a sense, Rockwell came into his creative powers at a time when new audiences, technologies, and markets were opening up. Residing in New Rochelle, New York in 1916, Rockwell sold his first cover work to the *Saturday Evening Post* – the nation's most popular magazine and a prized commission for a young illustrator. Mass-circulated national magazines with great popularity catapulted certain artists, particularly Rockwell, into millions of households weekly. He clearly had the right talent at the right time and became the most beloved and popular illustrator in America.

Constantly seeking new ideas and new faces in his daily life, Rockwell wrote that everything he had ever seen or done had gone into his pictures. He painted not only the scenes and people close to him but in a quest for authenticity, would approach total strangers and ask them to model. His internal art of 'storytelling' integrated with his external skills as an artist, merged into an incredible facility to judge the perfect moment at which to stop the action … and capture it on canvas. The elements which defined and embellished a story were in place. His covers were a whole story portrayed within a single image-it is what sold the magazines.

Top (from left to right): Interior views of Ballroom, Tiffany Loggia and Grand Salon, NMAI, Newport, RI
Bottom: Aerial view of the National Museum of American Illustration at Vernon Court on Bellevue Ave.

In the 1940s, Rockwell moved to Arlington, Vermont, where he painted the full canvases which are increasingly treasured by collectors today. With artist Grandma Moses as a neighbor and local townspeople as his models, Rockwell became a living part of Americana – a national treasure, and today an iconic figure with his name even used as an adjective, 'Rockwellian.'

Throughout his lifetime he flourished as an artist/illustrator, but he well realized that within the framework of being an illustrator he was not considered an artist by the fine art establishment. Rockwell always remained acutely aware of his goals as an artist and his lack of critical acceptance.

Interestingly in the 1960's, living in Stockbridge, Massachusetts, Rockwell struck out in a new direction. Though by that time his reputation was rooted in the evocation of nostalgia, he boldly tackled political issues. His work, *The Problem We All Live With* (page 151), confronted America's racial tensions. *The Russian Schoolroom* (page 154), showed the demonic Communist discipline with its confining dictatorial regime, a bust of Lenin, and a single student looking in the other direction and quite possibly dreaming of another way. Perhaps that student was a Mikhail Gorbachev? Near the end of his career, Rockwell painted Presidents Kennedy, Eisenhower, Nixon, and Johnson as well as portraits of other world leaders, including Nehru of India.

Today, Norman Rockwell is larger than life. His works are recognized worldwide and his name used universally to describe a lifestyle and an era considered distinctly American.

Norman Rockwell once said:

> *No man with a conscience can just bat out illustrations. He's got to put all of his talent, all of his feelings into them. If illustration is not considered art, then that is something that we have brought upon ourselves by not considering ourselves artists. I believe that we should say, 'I am not just an illustrator, I am an artist.'*

Judy Goffman Cutler
Laurence S. Cutler AIA RIBA
National Museum of American Illustration
Newport, Rhode Island, US

Winter 2010

National Museum of American Illustration

The National Museum of American Illustration, founded in 1998, is located at Vernon Court (1898), a Beaux-Arts adaptation of an early 18th century French chateau designed by the noted architects Carrére & Hastings. It is the first national museum devoted exclusively to American illustration art.

Illustration is artwork created to be reproduced in books, magazines, newspapers and advertisements. Paintings by such luminaries as Norman Rockwell, Maxfield Parrish, J.C. Leyendecker, Charles Dana Gibson, NC Wyeth, and 80 other illustrators are displayed in a "Gilded Age" mansion, creating a unique union of art and architecture. The Museum is administered by the American Civilization Foundation, a nonprofit organization with the goal to educate and enlighten the global public in an appropriate venue for appreciating the greatest collection of illustration art: *"the most American of American art."*

DULWICH PICTURE GALLERY

Dulwich Picture Gallery was founded in 1811. It was England's first purpose-built public art gallery, designed by the period's greatest architect, Sir John Soane (1754-1837). Its founders, Noel Desenfans, Francis Bourgeois and Margaret Desenfans, lie to this day in the beautiful mausoleum in the heart of the Gallery. Dulwich's Collection provides a perfect introduction to art in the age of Baroque. Its outstanding collection of 17th and 18th century Old Master paintings makes this remarkable and picturesque place one of the glories of Europe: Rembrandt, Rubens, Canaletto, Poussin, Gainsborough, Hogarth, Reni, Guercino, Raphael, Tiepolo, amongst many other famous names are all represented by masterpieces at Dulwich. The year 2011 marks Dulwich's 200th Anniversary. It is the oldest public art gallery in the United Kingdom.

Dulwich director's Statement

Rockwell is terrific. It's become too tedious to pretend he isn't.

*S*o famously wrote *The New Yorker* art critic Peter Schjedahl in *Art News*, September 1999. I could not agree more. My epiphany with Rockwell occurred before that, at one of the great exhibitions of his work which periodically circle the United States. But one should not underestimate the strength of anti-Rockwell feeling that existed just a few years ago– and indeed still exists in some circles. As a 'Brit' with very little in the way of qualifications to justify my commenting on another country's idiosyncrasies, I can only assume that it has something to do with what you might call 'brand America.' Norman Rockwell's America must have seemed like a travesty to those who saw the grittier 'truth' about the 'land of the free' in issues like the wars in Korea and Vietnam, and the civil rights struggle (although Rockwell did, of course, tackle the latter issue in paintings such as *The Problem We All Live With*, the vivid study for which is displayed here). To the Woodstock generation, Rockwell's images were, simply, lies – and 'Rockwellian' a term of abuse. To which, the only possible answer must be a very American, "Lighten UP!"

Of his greatness as an illustrator, there can be no doubt. The extreme reactions to his work are in a way testimony to that. His sunny, occasionally sentimental images of American life would not make some people so very angry, if it were not for the fact that they palpably resonate with real life. Film-makers Steven Spielberg and George Lucas love and collect his work (and many of his illustrations remind me of that other great American film-maker of an earlier era, Frank Capra) and that should be no surprise, because they are supreme storytellers too. In fact, the extent to which Rockwell's imagery has fed into cinema (and vice versa) is remarkable indeed – some stars (Doris Day? Jim Carrey? Steve Martin? Tom Hanks?) could have walked out of one of his illustrations in some of their roles, and much Hollywood comedy, particularly of the Frank Capra/Howard Hawks/Preston Sturges vintage, even today, reminds us of his ironic humour and idealised vision of America. A certain irony, then, that he should have provided the glossy, gorgeous portraits of the stars of Orson Welles' *The Magnificent Ambersons* (pages 94-95)– a film that dissects the American family archetype like no other. A brilliant, and presumably deliberate, marriage of contrasts - Welles provides the mould beneath Rockwell's cheese.

One of Rockwell's most special skills is his ability to heighten the comic moment to a point of universal recognition. What he illustrates are the stories of our lives as we like to tell them, rather than as they actually happened.

Top Left: Interior view of Soane Galleries, Dulwich Picture Gallery, London, England
Bottom Left: Aerial view of Dulwich Picture Gallery, London, England, Photo by Simon Hoare

If you watch an animated conversation on the street, it is easy to see, amongst all the "he saids" and "then she saids", how we all like to dramatise these dreary everyday stories with comic double-takes that were never made, sometimes with extreme faces of disbelieving shock or uncontrolled hilarity, or devastating one-liners that we did not think of until later. This is the very stuff of Norman Rockwell's art; a perfect example of this is the blissful sketch of a *Breakfast Table Political Argument* (page 123). A ranting husband, stubborn young wife, bawling child; every one of us can relate to the situation and laugh at similar moments in our own lives. This is what made him so extraordinary an illustrator particularly for the cover of the *Saturday Evening Post* – he exalted everyman, made us all funnier than we are, while observing us in such extraordinary detail that these vignettes seemed truer than reality.

The exhibition is full of examples of this talent. Observe the *Volunteer Fireman* (page 75): here is a simple truth, presented in the most entertaining and decorative manner. The boy sees the fire just as an exciting adventure; the fireman sees the fire as the potentially grim tragedy it undoubtedly could become; the dog - what fire? It's all about the running and barking. Funny, definitely – but serious underneath, and as perfect in its design as any medieval coat of arms. The realism of detail, as always with Rockwell, is marvellous – the untied old boots, the battered leather slippers, the notched axe, the light of the fire reflected on faces and clothes.

His virtuosity in capturing observed detail is one aspect of his art that should make us look long and seriously at the paintings behind the illustrations. Just as with one of his colleagues, N.C. Wyeth, paintings by whom graced the walls of Dulwich Picture Gallery during the Summer of 2010 as part of the exhibition, *The Wyeths: Three Generations of American Art*, from the Bank of America Merrill Lynch Collection, Rockwell could certainly handle oil paint like an Old Master. His paintings, once seen simply as a means to an end (the printed illustration), have been rediscovered comparatively recently, and now fetch fabulous sums on the market.

Furthermore, he studied those Old Masters, and learned from them. At Dulwich Picture Gallery, there are works from the 17th century Dutch School that speak something very like the same language. A small gem like Pieter Nys's *A Woman Spinning* also depends for its impact on that exact rendering of human interaction, married to a wealth of lovingly-observed domestic detail. A similar kind of comic exaggeration can be found in the exquisite little paintings of Adriaen van Ostade. The point need not be laboured; but Rockwell's famous *Shuffleton's Barbershop* (page 129) reminds me, in the subtlety of its play of light and its strong evocation of place, at the very least of our own Gerrit Dou, *Woman Playing a Clavichord* (page 62); and that painting influenced Jan Vermeer, of whose work Rockwell was well aware.

This exhibition is bracketed by two rooms dedicated to one of his great monuments – all 323 covers that he did for the *Saturday Evening Post*, an achievement that above all else embedded him in the American consciousness. Included are early quasi-Victorian genre pieces, Presidential portraits, wonderful visual jokes, everyone's favourite Santas, whimsical insights into the human condition, and serious, heartfelt patriotism. Here, if anywhere, is *Norman Rockwell's America* - and who wouldn't want to live there?

To Laurence Cutler and Judy Goffman Cutler, founding Directors of the National Museum of American Illustration, I wish to give my most sincere thanks. Their visit to Dulwich Picture Gallery to see the *Walter Sickert in Venice* show in 2009 led to a rapid meeting of minds, and the first of many laughs, in Gallery X, with our Dutch Italianate paintings as a backdrop. A Rockwell show had long been a dream of mine – and here, suddenly, Laurence and Judy offered an opportunity to achieve it. They responded with enthusiasm, and I appreciate enormously all the effort that they have undertaken to make my dream come about.

At Dulwich my thanks go to Mella Shaw, Head of Exhibitions, and to Lizzie Watson, Exhibitions Officer, for their co-ordination of this project. The show was made possible at Dulwich with the assistance of the Government Indemnity Scheme provided by the Department of Culture, Media and Sport, administered by the MLA.

We are enormously grateful to *The Wall Street Journal Europe* and Virgin Atlantic, both of whom have been partnership sponsors of this exhibition. We also owe sincere thanks to the Embassy of the United States of America, to Curtis Publishing for their generous sponsorship, and to another sponsor who wishes to remain anonymous. Finally, as so often, the Friends of Dulwich Picture Gallery have most generously supported this exhibition; along with the American Friends of Dulwich Picture Gallery. My grateful thanks to both.

Ian A C Dejardin
Dulwich Picture Gallery
London, England

Winter 2010

Norman Rockwell's TIMELINE

First *Boys' Life* cover
1913

First *Post* cover
1916

First *Country Gentleman* cover
1917

First *Collier's* cover
1919

1910 NR leaves Mamaroneck High School to attend the National Academy of Design in New York City

1911 NR enrolls at the Art Students League to take classes with George Bridgman and Thomas Fogarty

1912 First works are published in C.H. Claudy's *Tell Me Why – Stories about Mother Nature* and Gabrielle Jackson's *Maid of Middies' Haven*

1912 Rockwell rents his first studio above a bordello in New York City

1913 First cover for *Boys' Life* magazine (see above); Receives position as Art Editor specializing in children's illustrations

1914 Participates in his first group exhibition at the New Rochelle Art Association

1915 **Moves to New Rochelle, New York;** establishes studio with Clyde Forsythe, cartoonist and illustrator

1916 First *Saturday Evening Post* cover published (May 20) (see above); Launches forty-seven year career with the *Post*; Marries Irene O'Connor

1917 First *Country Gentleman* cover (August 25) (see above)

1918 Enlists in the Navy and is stationed at the Naval Reserve Base, Charleston, South Carolina, during World War I; appointed United States Art Editor for Base publication, *Afloat & Ashore*; Publishes work in several major publications including *Judge* magazine

1919 First *Collier's* cover (March 1) (see above)

1894 Norman Percevel Rockwell (NR) is born on February 3rd to Nancy Hill and Jarvis Waring Rockwell in New York City

1907 NR and family move to a series of boarding houses in Mamaroneck, New York

1908 NR attends Mamaroneck High School and the Chase School of Art in the afternoons

1894 - 1909

1910 - 1919

1896 Supreme Court case Plessy v. Ferguson upholds the constitutionality of racial segregation

1898 Spanish American War begins (April 25) and ends (December 10); US gains Cuba, Puerto Rico, Guam and the Philippines

1901 Theodore Roosevelt becomes 26th President of the US after McKinley's assassination

1913 Woodrow Wilson is inaugurated as the 28th President of the US

1914 World War I begins in Europe between the Allied and Central Powers; Panama Canal opens

1917 US enters WWI on the side of the Allies (April 6)

1919 League of Nations meets for the first time (January 13); Treaty of Versailles is signed, ending WWI (June 28)

WORLD EVENTS

First Full Color *Post* Cover
February 6, 1926

Lindbergh on *Post* cover
July 23, 1927

Rockwell with oldest son, Jarvis

1922 NR is selected by JC Leyendecker to be a judge in Miss America Pageant

1922-23, 1927, 1929 NR frequently travels throughout Europe, South and North America with friends and fellow artists

1925 First Boy Scout calendar; Scout commissions continue until 1976

1926 Rockwell's first four color *Post* cover, *The Old Sign Painter* (February 6)(see above, left)

1930 Thirteen year marriage to Irene O'Connor ends in divorce; Journeys to California to visit Clyde Forsythe; meets and marries Mary Barstow in California

1931 A son, Jarvis Waring Rockwell, is born (see above)

1932, 1938 NR travels through Europe

1933 A second son, Thomas Rhodes Rockwell, is born

1935 Receives commission to illustrate Mark Twain's *Tom Sawyer* (1936) and *Huckleberry Finn* (1940)

1936 A third son, Peter Barstow Rockwell, is born

1939 Rockwell family moves to Arlington, Vermont

1920 - 1929

1930 - 1939

1927 Charles Lindbergh makes first solo nonstop transatlantic flight (May 20)(See Rockwell's *Post* cover above, right)

1929 Herbert Hoover is inaugurated as the 31st President of the US

1929 Stock market crash begins the Great Depression worldwide (October 29)

1933 President Franklin D. Roosevelt enacts the New Deal to begin recovery from the Great Depression (March)

1939 Germany invades Poland; World War II begins in parts of Europe (September 1)

Clockwise from Top Left:
Rockwell's sons pose with Victor Mature on set of Cecil B. DeMille's *Samson and Delilah,* 1948; Rockwell posing with *Post* cover models for *Breaking Home Ties,* 1954; Rockwell painting *The Toss,* 1950; President Eisenhower portrait, October 11, 1952 *Post* cover; Rockwell's sketch of his studio burning, 1943

1941-1946 Rockwell paints the Willie Gillis series for *The Post*

1943 Rockwell and Mead Schaeffer bring ideas for paintings to the US Government which are rejected; Rockwell promotes his idea to *Post* editor, Ben Hibbs, and *The Four Freedoms* are printed and distributed, ultimately raising $132 million for the war effort

1943 Rockwell's Arlington studio burns down

1943-1944 Ken Stuart takes over as art editor of *The Post*

1946 Arthur L. Guptill publishes *Norman Rockwell Illustrator,* the first monograph on the artist

1948 Rockwell is a founder of the Famous Artists School in Westport, CT

1952 Rockwell paints a portrait of President Eisenhower and then paints presidential candidates every four years (see above)

1953 Rockwell and his family move to Stockbridge, MA

1959 Mary Rockwell dies unexpectedly of a heart attack

1940 - 1949

1950 - 1959

1941 After Japan attacks at Pearl Harbor, US enters WWII against Japan, Germany and Italy (December)

1945 US, under President Truman, drop atomic bombs on Hiroshima and Nagasaki; Japan surrenders, ending the war (August 6 and 9)

1945 United Nations is established (October)

1947 Jackie Robinson becomes the first African American Major League Baseball player

1949 NATO (North Atlantic Treaty Organization) is established with 12 founding members

1950 Communist North Korea invades South Korea, starting the Korean War (June)

1953 Armistice is signed, ending Korean War (July)

1954 Supreme Court case Brown v. Board of Education of Topeka rules racial segregation in school systems to be unconstitutional

1956 France exits Vietnam, US supports South Vietnam in conflict

1957 President Eisenhower sends federal troops to Little Rock, Arkansas to enforce racial integration in schools (September)

1958 First American satellite, Explorer I, is launched

Clockwise from Top Left:
Rockwell's last Post cover, December 14, 1963; Rockwell in costume as "Busted Flush" on the set of Stagecoach, 1965; Mary and Norman Rockwell; NR's last published work, American Artist cover 1976; Rockwell painting studies for Post cover, The Connoisseur, January 13, 1962

1960 *My Adventures as an Illustrator*, Rockwell's memoir, is published and serialized in the *Post*

1961 Marries retired teacher Molly Punderson

1963 Rockwell ends 47 year association with *The Saturday Evening Post* (final cover shown above)

1964 Starts 10 year relationship with *Look* magazine; Focuses on deeper concerns and personal interests

1973 Establishes a trust to preserve his artistic legacy

1976 Adds his studio and contents to his trust

1976 Rockwell's last magazine cover is published by *American Artist* (see above)

1977 Norman Rockwell is awarded the Presidential Medal of Freedom by President Ford

1978 Dies on November 8th in Stockbridge, MA, at 84

1960 - 1969

1970 - 1978

1962 John Glenn orbits the Earth; Cuban Missile Crisis launches naval blockade of Cuba

1963 Rev. Martin Luther King, Jr. delivers 'I Have a Dream' speech (Aug. 28); President Kennedy is assassinated (Nov. 22)

1964 President Johnson signs the Civil Rights Act

1968 Rev. Martin Luther King, Jr. is assassinated (April 4); Sen. Robert F. Kennedy is assassinated (June 5)

1969 Astronauts Neil Armstrong and Edwin Aldrin are first to walk on the moon

1974 Nixon resigns from Presidency after Watergate scandal; Vice President Gerald R. Ford becomes President (August)

1975 President Ford removes all US officials and aid from Saigon; ends Vietnam War (April)

NEW ROCHELLE, NEW YORK
1913-1939

*N*orman Rockwell (NR), by the age of 19, was Art Editor for *Boys' Life* magazine published by the Boy Scouts of America. Such an early success coupled with a unique painting style launched his career. In 1915, Rockwell and illustrator Clyde Forsythe rented a studio with famed sculptor Frederic Remington in New Rochelle, formalizing their professional activities in earnest. A year later, he landed his first cover for the nation's most popular magazine, the *Saturday Evening Post* (May 20, 1916; see page 164). His popular image for that first *Post* cover became the prototype for his classic Norman Rockwell magazine covers. The astonishing amount of the *Post* commission of $75 per cover enabled him to comfortably marry his sweetheart, a schoolteacher, Irene O'Connor. Additional financial security came quickly due to his continued successful images for *Boys' Life* and the *Post*. These on-going commissions gave him a newfound self-confidence to market his talent. Six more *Post* covers immediately followed, along with illustrations for other important magazines of the era: *Country Gentleman*, *Judge*, *Life*, and *Literary Digest*.

By 1917, NR had such a variety of clients it enabled him to settle full-time in New Rochelle, NY – a small town with a notable artist population including Charles Dana Gibson, Coles Phillips, and the Leyendecker brothers, Frank and J. C. (Joe). NR idolized Joe and considered him to be "the best illustrator." Yet, after all was said and done, it was Rockwell's *Post* covers that were the most widely distributed with their circulation increasing whenever one of his covers appeared. Delighted with this success, his goal was to share his art with millions, unlike other artists, who had precious few viewing their works. NR had the distinction of being published as soon as a painting was completed and it generated instant gratification for this illustrator. His images were omnipresent and his work well-recognized by the public. He was perhaps the first ubiquitous artist.

In 1930, after returning from one of his European jaunts, he and Irene divorced. Their years together were absorbed by NR's quest for success and it clearly affected their marriage. It prompted him to try to change his life coupled with a renewed determination to further his professional career. In 1930, he left for California to visit his former studio-mate Clyde Forsythe and whilst there, met his second wife, Mary Barstow. It was during this trip that he painted the movie star Gary Cooper for a *Post* cover. After marrying, the couple returned to New Rochelle. Thereafter, he rapaciously devoted himself to creating images of America for every magazine and advertising commission that came his way. His fame had reached Gary Cooper's movie star status and his income soared.

Between 1931-1936, Rockwell's family expanded to include three boys, Jarvis, Thomas and Peter. He virtually fathered three in-house models, spawning new inspiration and more boyhood dilemmas for him to characterize with paint and canvas. Nearing the end of the difficult Great Depression decade in 1939, along with many of his art contemporaries, Rockwell relocated to Arlington, Vermont. He moved in search of a new environment to shed Depression woes.

Opposite: Detail from Norman Rockwell's *Till the Boys Come Home*

ARLINGTON, VERMONT
1939 - 1953

*N*orman Rockwell moved with Mary and their three sons to Arlington where he quickly made local friends and later illustrators; John Atherton and Mead Schaffer moved there as well. His *Post* magazine work immediately reflected a change in style, perhaps influenced by his new rural lifestyle. His works became less stereotypical and posed and he abandoned his trademark circle used in earlier *Post* covers. He incorporated more details and his humor was more subtle, but still poignant. NR's Arlington days marked a whole new direction for his career, while World War II overshadowed everything.

In 1942, Ben Hibbs took over as Editor for the *Post* and NR developed a new relationship with the magazine. With the onset of WWII, he painted servicemen on *Post* covers, but in his inimitable way. While others depicted the horrors of war, he painted his first Willie Gillis, a personification of the American soldier. Willie Gillis ultimately appeared on 11 covers of the *Post* which chronicled his exploits (see examples on page 90). He also illustrated sailors, marines, and soldiers both at their jobs and at home on leave, never showing blood and gore. Always optimistic, yet unhappy with himself, his images appealed to the hearts of Americans while maintaining Rockwellian charm. In 1942, Rockwell painted the famous *Four Freedoms* (pages 102-109). He originally pitched the idea to the US Government, but they could not afford them at that time. On his way back from Washington, he stopped in Philadelphia to show the idea to Hibbs, who immediately recognized the importance of the four artworks. Inspired by President Franklin D. Roosevelt's 1941 speech, they became a huge success in the US as well as abroad. The images affirmed the values and beliefs which signified Norman Rockwell's America. The posters became part of a war campaign and the originals toured across the country to raise money for the war bond effort. Yet he was getting more depressed than he had been in 1932, a decade earlier.

In the very next year, Rockwell's studio burned to the ground destroying 28 years of his favorite artworks and invaluable reference materials. It was a difficult moment for the artist, but one which allowed a fresh start under a new *Post* Art Editor, Ken Stuart. He relocated his family from Arlington to West Arlington and continued to use locals as models, immortalizing them on *Post* covers. The Arlington stamp on his work was indelible. His years there marked a prosperous time and some of his best artworks. However he needed help to deal with his and Mary's depression and in 1953, the family moved to Stockbridge, Massachusetts. That move was generated by the Austen Riggs Center, where he sought treatment for Mary's alcoholism and for his own depression. Mary also received shock therapy at the Institute for Living in Hartford, Connecticut. In 1959, Mary had a heart attack and passed away in her sleep. This began an even darker period in Rockwell's life where painting became an outlet for his grief; portraying happiness while suffering his own unhappiness, his work took on more serious undertones.

Opposite: Detail from Norman Rockwell's *April Fools - Girl with Shopkeeper* (page 119)

STOCKBRIDGE, MASSACHUSETTS
1953-1978

*N*orman and Mary Rockwell had spent some years clouded in depression while she suffered from alcoholism. Prior to settling in Stockbridge, Massachusetts, they commuted from Arlington, Vermont, to avail themselves of Eric Erikson, Harvard Professor of Psychiatry, the world's most noted psychoanalyst and on the staff of the local Austen Riggs sanitarium. NR's and Prof. Erikson's relationship evolved into a lasting friendship. Erikson's obituary stated "after Freud, no single psychoanalyst has more profoundly influenced world culture and society... the most widely influential in the total socio-historical surround...." Rockwell's long term depression is a revelation to most of his admirers for their beloved creator of an idealized America was long beleaguered with depression. Almost unfathomable to contemplate, he rose above his problems and expressed happiness in images he painted of others, for others to appreciate. After 30 years of marriage, Mary died of a heart attack in 1959.

In 1961, Rockwell married Molly Punderson, a former schoolteacher at Milton Academy reitred and living in Stockbridge. The couple shared a passion for world events and social change in counter-distinction to his two previous wives. In the meanwhile, the *Post* commissioned NR to paint portraits of important, international political figures, such as Presidents Nixon and Kennedy, and leaders like Nehru of India and Nasser of Egypt. However, NR wanted to paint only those whom he admired and while he adored Kennedy, he did not like Nixon, as one example. In the early 1960s, world, national and local issues took on more importance. Like so many others, Rockwell became increasingly interested in politics and the importance of social responsibility in the world community. Perhaps his three young sons prevailed upon him to broaden his outlook even further. In 1963, after 47 years with the *Saturday Evening Post*, Rockwell painted his last *Post* cover. He began working with *Look* magazine and they allowed this superstar of the magazine cover to address current affairs. He had the latitude to select subjects which he felt mattered more than portraits of topical political personages. His later works included *The Problem We All Live With* (see page 151) concerning the desegregation of schools in the South. He expanded an already prolific travel schedule seeking subjects and knowledge, and painted the Peace Corps in Ethiopia in action, NASA space program, and Russian schoolchildren. A distinct departure from the *Post*, this marked another beginning and another milestone period in his career.

In 1968, Rockwell, his wife Molly, and a local group converted the historic Stockbridge Old Corner House into a small museum to which Rockwell gifted many of his works. The Museum then helped with the first Rockwell retrospective exhibition organized by New York's Dannenberg Gallery. The exhibition was enormously popular, prompting a countrywide tour. In 1977, President Gerald Ford presented the United States of America's Presidential Medal of Freedom to Norman Percevel Rockwell. A year later, he passed away at his home in Stockbridge at the age of 84. His legacy continues to grow exponentially. Today, Norman Rockwell is considered America's preeminent artist/illustrator, perhaps our greatest storyteller, and the world's most beloved illustrator.

Opposite: Detail from Norman Rockwell's *Choir Boy Combing Hair for Easter* (page 135)

Above and Right:
Norman Rockwell's Paint Box which was used
from 1910 - 1930.
Wooden art box, palette and paint brushes
Stenciled 'N. Rockwell' on outside cover.
This paint box is thought to be the derivation of
his famous stencil-like signature.

ARTWORKS IN THE EXHIBITION
THE ROCKWELL ART BEHIND THE ADJECTIVE
'ROCKWELLIAN'

NORMAN ROCKWELL
*THE FISHERMAN
1916, oil on canvas
24" x 16", signed lower left "N P Rockwell"
Recreation magazine, May 1916 cover

Rockwell painted only three covers for *Recreation,* a magazine that appealed to an audience similar to *Boys' Life.* Both magazines' illustrations typically featured popular outdoor activities. This early cover, painted when Norman was just 22 years old, includes the date (1916) and his middle initial "P" for Percevel, which he dropped the very next year (see detail below). Rockwell's signature style of his later covers is noticeably absent from this work, but this painting shows his early interest in a painterly technique, much like Howard Pyle.

Left:
Another example of a *Recreation* magazine cover by Rockwell, September 1917

Below:
Detail of signature 'N P Rockwell 1916' from *The Fisherman* with the rarity of initial 'P'

NORMAN ROCKWELL
COUSIN REGINALD PLAYS PIRATES
1917, oil on canvas on board
30" x 30", signed lower right
Country Gentleman, November 3, 1917 cover

NORMAN ROCKWELL
✳ ***COUSIN REGINALD UNDER THE MISTLETOE***
1917, oil on canvas
22" x 22", signed lower right
Country Gentleman, December 22, 1917 cover

As Rockwell was beginning his career, he uniformly incorporated children into most of his published works. An example was the ongoing adventures and misfortunes of Cousin Reginald, a popular theme and character for Rockwell's *Country Gentleman* magazine covers. Cousin Reginald, modeled by Claude Fitzhugh, was an arrogant, yet harmless city boy who was often made the target of pranks by his country cousins. In *Cousin Reginald Plays Pirates* (see top right), Reginald and his mischievous relatives, Chuck Peterkin and the Doolittle brothers, are pictured playing pirates. Cousin Reginald is tied up and being charged by Rusty Doolittle while his brother Tubby and Chuck assist with menacing glares. In the background, their dog Patsy observes the mischief. Today such seemingly harmless antics are taken more seriously and considered 'bullying.'

In *Cousin Reginald Under the Mistletoe* (see bottom right), his cousin, Rusty Doolittle, is pushing Reginald to kiss a ready and able girl under the mistletoe at a holiday party. Rockwell deftly captures the essence of the scene with the girl's lips puckered and hands resting impatiently on her hips while the blushing Reginald cowers away. This painting was the seventh in a series featuring Cousin Reginald spanning two years for *Country Gentleman*. The magazine appealed to a different audience for its publisher, Curtis Publishing Company, also publisher of *The Saturday Evening Post*, which boasted a more diverse readership.

NORMAN ROCKWELL
UNCLE SAM
1918, oil on canvas
29" x 21", signed lower right
Red Cross magazine, April, 1918 cover

Rockwell's *Uncle Sam* painted for the cover of *Red Cross* magazine shows him parading and protecting the children who also needed help during World War I. This is one of the few artworks where Rockwell depicts a wilderness landscape in colors which are perhaps more reminiscent of NC Wyeth than Rockwell. As it is an early cover, he experiments in creating the effect of a setting sun with a virtual rainbow of colors in the background. Rockwell created only four magazine covers for the Red Cross, three of which were influenced by the ongoing World War I.

NORMAN ROCKWELL
PETTICOATS AND PANTS
1918, oil on canvas
26 1/4" x 22", signed lower right
Judge magazine, June 1, 1918 cover

Between 1917 and 1919, *Judge*, a popular humor magazine, published six Rockwell covers including *Petticoats and Pants*. Completed at the very cusp of Rockwell's career, it was published a month after Germany failed to halt US troops from crossing the Atlantic in the midst of World War I. *Petticoats and Pants* is a charming example of two distinctive fashion statements amongst the opposite sexes at a time when fashion was not considered important. However, those differing fashions calmly blended on the cover of *Judge* magazine, and emerged as a witty and unique Rockwellian juxtaposition. Thenceforth, many of Rockwell's images feature similar comparisons of incongruous ideas, which when conjoined, harmonized to create ironic and comedic views of the world. This technique of contrasting subject matters would become a regular occurrence in Rockwell's oeuvre, whether it is a naive young boy and an experienced firefighter racing to action in *Volunteer Fireman* (1931; p. 75), or the optimistic college graduate headed into a world with headlines exclaiming the terrors and problems of the world, as in *Boy Graduate* (1959; p. 141), four decades later.

Judge

NORMAN ROCKWELL
*TILL THE BOYS COME HOME
1918, oil on canvas
29 1/2" x 23 1/2", signed lower right
Life magazine, August 15, 1918 cover

Rockwell often chose to illustrate those people who were overlooked by society. During a time when most illustrators were focusing on soldiers fighting in World War I, Rockwell instead paid tribute to those people left behind. Here he depicts four young, forlorn ladies trying to distract themselves with knitting and contemplation, while it is clear their true thoughts are only of their men at war. In Rockwell's painting, each detail is significant to the overall theme. For example, he includes a piece of censored mail from a soldier (see bottom center of the composition). It is a subtle reminder of the difficulties families and loved ones experienced in an age when much less information was available to the public than now. Communication other than mail was nil.

"TILL THE BOYS COME HOME"

NORMAN ROCKWELL
KAYNEE BLOUSES AND WASH SUITS MAKE YOU LOOK ALL DRESSED UP
1919, oil on canvas
21 1/2" x 19 1/2", initialed lower left
Boys' Life advertisement, November, 1919

In this painting, Norman Rockwell has captured wide-eyed, youthful exuberance in the form of two dapper young boys and puppy. Both young men stand proudly and erect, meeting the viewer's gaze. The boys are framed by an oval shape, which is repeated in the subjects' faces. The use of the oval shape was a technique which clearly shows Leyendecker's influence on Norman Rockwell. It was a stylistic theme Leyendecker often used particularly in his Arrow Collar advertisements.

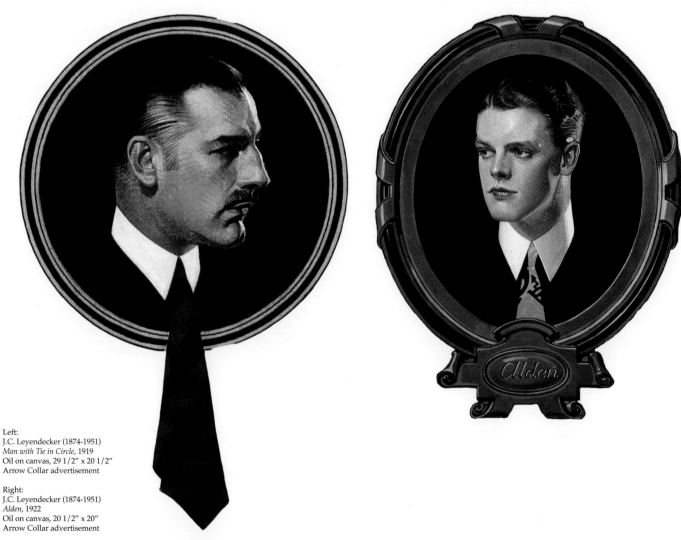

Left:
J.C. Leyendecker (1874-1951)
Man with Tie in Circle, 1919
Oil on canvas, 29 1/2" x 20 1/2"
Arrow Collar advertisement

Right:
J.C. Leyendecker (1874-1951)
Alden, 1922
Oil on canvas, 20 1/2" x 20"
Arrow Collar advertisement

NORMAN ROCKWELL
THE DOUGHBOY AND HIS ADMIRERS
1919, oil on canvas
24 1/2" x 21 1/2", signed lower left
Saturday Evening Post, February 22, 1919 cover

The theme of patriotism is consistently present in Rockwell's illustrations. During World War I, ineligible for active duty, he served in the United States Naval Reserve Force for a short period. In addition to producing illustrations for the Navy, Rockwell's support for the war is evident in each magazine cover he created of American servicemen. In *The Doughboy and His Admirers*, the group of children are proudly surrounding the hero returning home. It is a reflection of the joy and happiness the entire country felt at the end of World War I.

NORMAN ROCKWELL
FIRST SHAVE
1919, oil on canvas
21" x 18", signed lower right
Farm and Fireside, April, 1919 cover

First Shave is one of five illustrations Rockwell completed between 1918 and 1922 for the cover of *Farm and Fireside, The National Farm Magazine.* Many of these covers focused on a country boy's memories of fishing, hiking, swinging, being scolded by father, and of course, shaving for the first time. Similar to the characters of his *Country Gentleman* covers, Rockwell depicts this same young boy barefoot with suspenders and a tattered straw hat with a hole in the top. By using the same character multiple times, Rockwell encouraged the reader to develop a relationship with that boy (his model). Such a serialization usage brought readers back month after month to continue immersing themselves in the ongoing story. In *First Shave*, Rockwell focuses on the concentration and care this young boy takes with his straight razor, imitating older men whom he watched shave. This is an important moment in every boy's life where he learns how to become a man.

NORMAN ROCKWELL
SKATING RACE
1920, oil on canvas
28" x 25", signed lower left
Country Gentleman, February 28, 1920 cover

In *Skating Race*, featured on the cover of *Country Gentleman* February 28, 1920, Rockwell illustrates a familiar moment of boys and girls on skates around the globe. A young boy smiles at the viewer as he glides effortlessly past his competition, a heavier opponent who purses his lip in determination as he tries to win the race. This image, like many of Rockwell's images, captivates viewers who recall such a scene in their children's lives and their own childhoods. The unique Rockwellian element is the winning racer looking the viewer directly in the eyes. His expression indicates a proud moment where skill, gumption and body weight, win the race. The winner invites the viewer to share in his success.

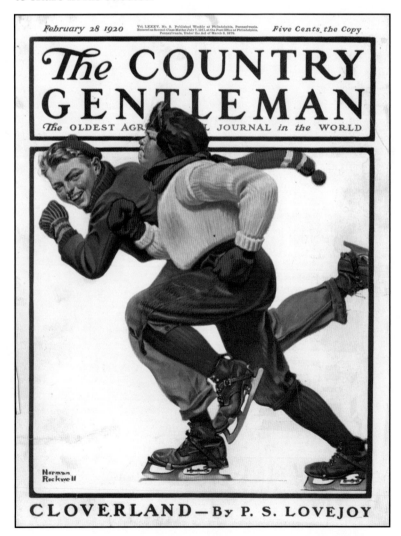

NORMAN ROCKWELL
THE PARTY AFTER THE PARTY
1922, oil on canvas
30" x 26", signed lower right
Edison Mazda advertisement, 1922
Ladies' Home Journal, June 1922, p. 87

This work was commissioned for Edison Mazda as a light bulb advertisement. Ultimately, Edison Mazda became General Electric and much of their early success was attributed to illustrations utilizing light as a theme on millions of calendars in Barber shops, gas stations, doctors' offices, and the like. In this painting, Rockwell uses the soft, warm glow of a lone lamp, a single bulb, to highlight the elderly woman and young girl. The woman listens attentively as the girl recounts the details of a party she attended earlier in the evening. Both figures are posed in a dynamic diagonal layout, emphasizing the intimacy of their conversation and drawing the reader's eye to the lamp as the focal point.

NORMAN ROCKWELL
THE RUNAWAY
1922, oil on canvas
36" x 24", signed lower right
Life magazine, June 1, 1922 cover

The Runaway shows Rockwell's ongoing interest in using a palette with broad, rich colors and thick impasto in the fashion of the Old Masters. Compare this work to those with a limited palette employed in earlier *Post* illustrations. A different, more painterly approach gave him the ability to create more detail with stronger shades and shadows, and a fully completed background. The fatherly clown offers tender consolation to the terrified boy with tears on each cheek, albeit pictured in the company of a smiling clown. In spite of his fears, the boy believed in the circus as a refuge from the real world, school, homework, and chores, yet he suddenly longs for home. He had dreams of an idyllic haven with wild animals and exotic travel, a life full of excitement and amusement, all but dispelled by unforeseen dangers and frightening challenges. A photographic portrait of Rockwell painting *The Runaway* was featured in a Devoe Artists' Materials advertisement in 1923 (page 52). It shows a Rembrandt reproduction hanging in the background, perhaps stimulating and reinforcing Rockwell's classical style and technique in this picture.

The Runaway

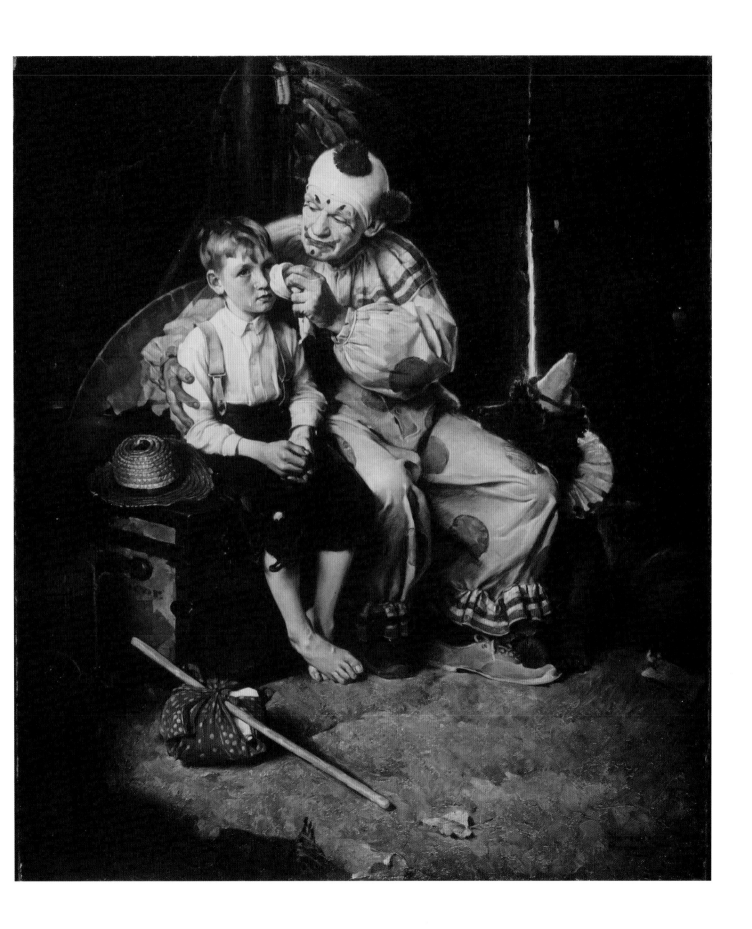

The photograph of Rockwell in his studio working on *The Runaway* (above) shows a reproduction of Rembrandt's *The Syndics* (opposite page, top). While certainly posed for advertisement purposes, this may not have been affectation on Rockwell's (or the advertiser's) part; the advertising text talks about the influence of Venetian painters, suggesting that the choice of the great Dutch master was Rockwell's own. Rockwell always acknowledged his debt to the Old Masters, particularly those of the Netherlandish 17th century coterie, whose interest in human relationships and truth chimed with his own preoccupations. While it might be too much to imply a direct quotation of Rembrandt's great masterpiece, Rockwell's *Young Valedictorian* (page 55) certainly shows him investigating similar issues – light, character, focus, and implied narrative.

Ian A C Dejardin

Top:
Rembrandt's *Syndics of the Draper's Guild*
1662, oil on canvas, 75.39" x 109.84"
Rijksmuseum, Amsterdam

Bottom:
Photograph of Norman Rockwell in his studio in
1922 with *The Runaway* on his easel and a print of
The Syndics on the opposite wall

★ 53

NORMAN ROCKWELL
YOUNG VALEDICTORIAN
c. 1922, oil on canvas
30" x 26", signed lower right

Young Valedictorian is a rare example of a finished Rockwell painting which remained unpublished. There is neither the usual irony nor humor present; it is simple matter of fact coupled with a certain tenderness. Although it is not known why it went unpublished, the painting remains an important and revealing example of Rockwell's development during the 1920s. Like *The Runaway* (page 51), it looks as if it had been painted by a European Old Master and not by an American illustrator. However, this painting does not surprise those familiar with Rockwell's extensive technical abilities, his stylistic treatment of subjects, or the various stages of his career. Others are astounded that the same artist could paint such a rich canvas while working simultaneously on others as diametrically different as *Threading the Needle* (1922; page 59).

This work particularly demonstrates Rockwell's facility with a paintbrush. He brought extraordinary talent in almost any style or period of fine art to the canvas at will, depending upon client and assignment.

NORMAN ROCKWELL
SANTA'S WORKSHOP
1922, oil on canvas
20 1/2″ x 16 1/2″, signed lower right
Western Newspaper Union advertisement,
The Clintonville Gazette, Clintonville, WI
December 14, 1922

Santa's Workshop re-visits Rockwell's youthful interest in pursuing the technical virtuosity of Old Master painters. A rich range of values and chiaroscuro effects are achieved with Rockwell's treatment of daylight pouring in from a window, onto Santa's snow-white, downy beard. Also evident is the artist's trademark ability to convey human emotion with the impact of a single facial expression – in this instance revealing Santa's joyful amusement at his accomplishment. These aforementioned qualities were manifested in many Rembrandt works. Both artists were unabashed humanists.

Above: Detail from Rembrandt, *A Girl at a Window*, 1645, oil on canvas, 81.6 x 66 cm
© By permission of the Trustees of Dulwich Picture Gallery

NORMAN ROCKWELL
THREADING THE NEEDLE
1922, oil on canvas
25 1/2" x 20 1/2", signed lower right
Saturday Evening Post, April 8, 1922 cover

Threading the Needle is prototypical of Rockwell's early *Saturday Evening Post* covers. He sometimes used a 'design system' that focused on a single, central item surrounded by an abstracted, simple white background. The cover's job was to sell magazines and Rockwell intuitively realized that meant to 'tell a whole story with a single image.' The model for this cover, Dave Campion, offered himself as a perfect Rockwell-type with his lanky, lean physique. In fact, he was so popular that the artist used him over again for many *Post* covers and advertisements.

NORMAN ROCKWELL
***MAN INSPECTING SOCKS**
1924, oil on masonite
23 1/2" x 23 1/2", signed lower left
Advertisement for Interwoven Socks,
Saturday Evening Post, August 9, 1924, p. 105

Rockwell began producing advertisements for Interwoven Socks in 1922. These ads were very successful and widely circulated in publications such as *American Magazine, The Saturday Evening Post,* and *Life. Man Inspecting Socks* is a clever depiction of a traveling businessman who, because of Interwoven, need never worry about holes in his socks while on the go. Additional clients for whom he illustrated advertisements included: Edison Mazda Lamp Works, Encyclopedia Britannica, Fisk Tire, Maxwell House Coffee, Overland Cars, Parker Pens, Dixon Ticonderoga Pencils, the Ford Motor Company, Listerine, Sun Maid Raisins, Post Cereals, Dutchess Trousers, and Coca-Cola.

NORMAN ROCKWELL
GOOD FOR ANOTHER GENERATION
1923, oil on canvas
36" x 30" framed, signed lower right
Lowe Brothers Co. advertisement
Saturday Evening Post, May 5, 1923, advertisement

Scenes of elderly couples were popular subjects for Norman Rockwell during the 1920s. In this illustration for Neptunite Varnish, he humorously conveys the idea that the varnish on the clock will most likely outlast the folks using it. According to the advertisement, the man applying the varnish is Colonel Dandle, a resident of New Rochelle, NY, who is very particular about the materials he uses in his home. Rockwell cleverly guides the viewer's eye from the paintbrush on the old grandfather clock, down the man's arm and directly to the product advertised, held in his wife's open palms. A successful graphic device both subtle and poignant, and the products sold well!

NORMAN ROCKWELL
*DREAMS IN THE ANTIQUE SHOP
1923, oil on canvas
36" x 30", signed lower right
Literary Digest, November 17, 1923 cover

In his series of cover paintings for *Literary Digest* magazine, Rockwell updated the concept of genre painting as well as developing a favorite theme during the five years he painted for that publication. *Dreams in the Antique Shop*, his second largest painting in the series, spotlights a lone girl surrounded by aged artifacts. She has paused while polishing a brass pot and gazes into space consumed with wistful thoughts. The expression on her face is a clear example of Dutch influence on Rockwell's technique. The girl exhibits a calm, stoic appearance similar to that of the woman in the Gerrit Dou painting below.

Above: Gerrit Dou, *A Woman Playing a Clavichord*, c. 1665, oil on panel, 14.84" x 11.73",
© By permission of the Trustees of Dulwich Picture Gallery

The image of a pretty young woman surrounded by domestic objects was a staple of 17th century Dutch genre painting, particularly associated with those artists known as the fijnschilders (fine painters). Based in Leiden, the first of the fijnschilders was Gerrit Dou. Dulwich Picture Gallery's *A Woman Playing a Clavichord* is one of his masterpieces. Far more successful in his lifetime than his master Rembrandt, Dou created several genre set-pieces that appear repeatedly in his own work, and in that of his followers, well into the 18th century (resurfacing later still as a primary source for Victorian genre painting). Our painting is the perfect example of this particular type. In Dutch terms, the objects surrounding the young woman would always hold special meaning: in the case of the Dulwich Dou, the flowers on the windowsill suggest spring and youth, the music book and the playing of the clavichord remind us of harmony, and through harmony, of love. Birdcages are often symbols of virginity – an open cage would imply that the bird has flown, so to speak. The cello and the wine glass remind us of the absent lover. Shakespeare provides the perfect epithet: 'If music be the food of love, play on...'.

Rockwell's young woman has been transposed to an antique shop, and she is surrounded by objects, but they have no allegorical or hidden significance. She may be dreaming of an absent boyfriend, but then again she might be musing over the price of vegetables. If we must look for a message, then it is in the suggestion of the imagination as the perfect escape from drudgery. So, there is no doubt that this is a different language – but much of the vocabulary is the same. The copper vessels, the ceramic jars, and above all, the sumptuous Turkish rug, all remind us that Rockwell was well aware of his sources, and in particular appreciated the virtuoso rendition of surfaces and still-life objects, just like his 17th century predecessors.

Ian A C Dejardin

Top Right: Detail (Reversed) from Rockwell's *Dreams in the Antique Shop*
Bottom Right: Detail from Gerrit Dou, *A Woman Playing a Clavichord*

NORMAN ROCKWELL
TIME TO RETIRE - SLEEPING TRAMP
1923, oil on canvas
28" x 21 1/4", signed and dated lower right
Fisk Tire advertisement
Country Life magazine, May 1924, p. 101

NORMAN ROCKWELL
*_TIME TO RETIRE - OLD MAN WITH SHOPPING
BASKET_*
1925, oil on canvas
32" x 26 1/2", signed lower right
Fisk Tire advertisement
Liberty magazine, February 28, 1925, p. 2

During the early 1920s, the Fisk Tire Company published a series of advertisements by Norman Rockwell, which capitalized on the double entendre of the Fisk "Time to Re-Tire" slogan. By depicting the sleeping character beneath a sign for Fisk Tires, Rockwell created another icon of American advertising using Fisk's company logo. *Sleeping Tramp* and *Old Man With Shopping Basket* demonstrate Rockwell's use of "outsider" characters during the twenties, when he began to incorporate sheriffs, hobos, and circus performers into his illustrations. Rockwell's portrayal of these characters remained sympathetic, preventing the illustrations from being mere "gags," and he usually added a touching element of humanity and sensibility to his humor. The realism and attention to detail in Rockwell's rendering of the men's accoutrements is evidence of the artist's classical training. Strong graphic elements, such as the orange sun and Fisk sign, indicate an early influence of Modernism into the design of his compositions. Altogether, these are two fine examples of the elements that made Rockwell's advertising art so successful and enduring.

NORMAN ROCKWELL
NO CHRISTMAS PROBLEM NOW - SANTA
WITH A PARKER PEN
1929, oil on canvas
28" x 23", signed lower right
Parker Duofold advertisement
Saturday Evening Post, December 14, 1929

Norman Rockwell adds a tongue-in-cheek element to this charming eyeshade portrayal of Santa Claus. With his placement of bookmarks in the advertisement itself (see below, left), the artist subtly indicates that girls are generally better behaved than boys. Santa's smirk-like expression with raised eyebrow reinforces that thought. Rockwell's depiction of Santa was such a popular and enduring image that for its 75th anniversary (1996), the Parker Pen company reissued a limited edition Duofold pen bearing Rockwell's signature with a medallion profile of the artist on the cap. The pen was packaged in a leather artist's case accompanied by a portfolio of six Rockwell Parker Pen advertisements, and this painting of Santa appeared on the masthead of an especially printed stationery.

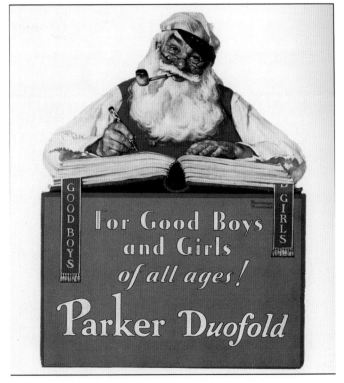

NORMAN ROCKWELL
CHRISTMAS - KNIGHT LOOKING IN STAINED GLASS WINDOW
1930, oil on canvas
44 1/4" x 34 1/4", signed lower right
Saturday Evening Post, December 6, 1930 cover

The Medieval knight is painted with related compositional props which each reinforce this image's historical context. Some defining elements are the stilted arch Gothic window, the Knight's armor, and the title 'Christmas' in a medieval-style font. Rockwell often drew from historical sources for inspiration and certainly one of his great professional strengths was a devotion to accuracy. A stilted arch is also seen in the *Choir Boy* (page 135), where Rockwell draws from ecclesiastical architecture to stage the image. In this picture, the white background serves to make the watchman (Knight) appear colder against the snuggly warmth and cheer within. The comfortable holiday revelers are apparently readying to feast while the lone guard is thrown asunder to 'do his job.' It is almost heart wrenching to note the warm interior glow reflecting on the knight's freezing face as he dutifully and longingly witnesses the holiday spirit of others.

Christmas

NORMAN ROCKWELL
THE SILHOUETTE
1931, oil on canvas
44" x 43 3/4", signed lower right
Ladies' Home Journal, February 1931, p. 14

Rockwell's *Ladies' Home Journal* illustrations were often fully developed and well detailed in contrast to his early *Saturday Evening Post* covers, which were vignettes with figures set against a stark white background. His subjects for the *Ladies' Home Journal* ranged from colonial era to modern day. *The Silhouette* illustrates a young colonial woman having her silhouette cut by an artist during the Revolutionary period. Instead of painting just the figures as one might see on a *Post* cover, Rockwell created an environment, a setting for the couple which places them at a specific time in history. The painting is filled with Revolutionary War details such as typical clothing, musket in corner, clock, as well as period furniture and the very architecture surrounding them. All props selected by the artist reinforce his message, his visual storytelling.

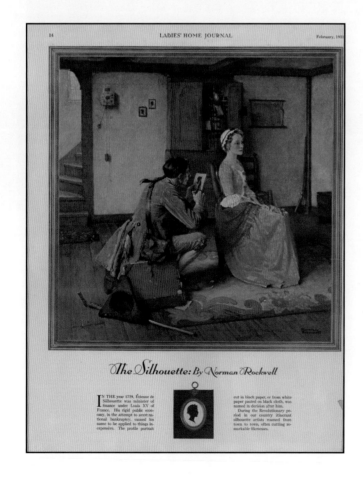

NORMAN ROCKWELL
VOLUNTEER FIREMAN
1931, oil on canvas
41" x 31", signed lower right
Saturday Evening Post, March 28, 1931 cover

The *Volunteer Fireman* was Rockwell's first and only attempt to create a painting using Dynamic Symmetry. This is an ancient Greek and Roman method for designing art and architecture with a proportional grid system which was derived from natural, geometric relationships. Rockwell had many notable artists whom he emulated, but two most especially: 1). the early *Post* cover illustrator JC Leyendecker, whom he called "The Master of the Magazine Cover"; and 2). the great illustrator of romance and fantasy images, Maxfield Parrish, who used this design system frequently. Rockwell understood the system and was impressed with the outcomes and successes achieved by Parrish. He tried it on this seminal work, but later declared it "too difficult and time-consuming" and never used it again. On the other hand, he used many of Leyendecker's other techniques and even subject matter for his magazine concepts, continually.

This painting portrays an eager young volunteer whose adrenaline is driving him along with the pure excitement of fire. He runs in stark contrast to the veteran whose experience leaves him determined to succeed in the face of danger, wholly unfazed by the naive youth's heroic ambitions, nor the dog simply 'along for the ride.'

NORMAN ROCKWELL
✷COUPLE WITH MILKMAN
1935, oil on canvas
27" x 30", signed lower right
Saturday Evening Post, March 9, 1935 cover

In the 1930s, Rockwell departed from his earlier focus of illustrating young children at play and older people at work to showing young adults. *Couple with Milkman* beautifully illustrates the Rockwell ideals of nostalgia and romance. The man and woman, both elegantly clad, have spent the entire night out with little concern for time. They do not realize how late it is until they bump into the milkman who is simply appalled at the wee hour of the morning for them to be returning. The milkman, depicted as an average guy, is disdainful and disgusted at the situation. The young lady is a bit shocked at the pocket watch, for she was having so much fun, time just disappeared. Rockwell characteristically obscured large parts of the well-known *Post* masthead with the image. This technique made his images appear to be more three-dimensional. Early *Post* covers always had the magazine name above two thick, horizontal black lines with the publication date and price in red between the lines. Only Rockwell could get away with such a blatant act of putting the artwork in a more important position than the name of the magazine – it was heretical. Rockwell's work and the *Post* itself ultimately became ubiquitous and everyone recognized the *Post* even with its name obliterated. Rockwell is at his best with scenes like this.

*NORMAN ROCKWELL
WILLIE TAKES A STEP
1935, oil on canvas
26" x 44", signed lower right
'Willie Takes a Step' by Don Marquis
American Magazine, January 1935
"We pitched at a county fair and Toby Bailey introduced me to a good
many artists of all kinds." p. 32-33

*NORMAN ROCKWELL
WILLIE TAKES A STEP - STUDY
1935, charcoal on paper
25 1/2" x 41 1/2", signed lower right

Norman Rockwell created *'Willie Takes a Step,'* for a short story published in *American Magazine.*
This painting, unlike a cover illustration, does not illustrate an entire story within a single
image. Rather, the artist must choose a single exciting scene from the story to entice the viewer
to continue to read the story to conclusion. In this image Willie, the boy standing at the front of
the table, has left home and joined a travelling circus. Rockwell chose to illustrate the moment
when Willie is introduced to all of the typical circus characters. The Circus Barker introduces
the ballerina, fat lady, trapeze artist, bearded lady (actually a man dressed as a woman), clown
and magician. The model who posed for Circus Barker was "Pops" Frederick, scion of a silent
screen family of stars (much like the Barrymores in later years) in the 20's and 30's. "Pops"
Frederick posed extensively for both Norman Rockwell and J.C. Leyendecker illustrations. In
'Willie Takes a Step,' even Pop's family dog 'Spot' makes an appearance, shown panting below
the picnic table bench.

Willie takes a step
By Don Marquis

THERE comes a time when every young fellow has got to strike out for himself, but I dilly-dallied around until I was fifteen years old before I become Foot-Loose.

The main trouble was Old Man Humphreys. He had been licking me since I was five years old every time his scinic excruciations bothered him or he ate something he couldn't digest or what he read in the papers disagreed with him. He got me from one of these orphan asylums in the State of Pennsylvania and moved me to a little town in Illinois to level on the edge of; and on account of the asylum being a citizen of an orator and me on one to church up to here there was no one to check up on him legal these lickings were.

I got very tired of Betty Hartley seeing him lick me so much, because she and I were practically engaged, having split a dime with a cold chisel. The Hartleys' house was right across the road from the Humphreys' farm, and the chances that girl had to see me licked were legion, as the books say.

So one day she sees to me she has got her doubts about me being a Hero, or any part of it. She says, "Would John Barry-

more or Wallace Beery let themselves be continually licked like that?"

"Yes," I says, making a snappy comeback, "you are always talking about John Barrymore or Wallace Beery. But I guess Clark Gable is the better actor of them all. He is a Head Guy. If Clark Gable would bounce a fist one of John Barrymore or Wallace Beery's chin you would see pretty darn' quick which is the better actor of the three!"

Betty is a very romantic girl on account of the reading master the sweatssize with. The Hartleys have got a whole room full of practically nothing but reading mater—old-time reading matter handed down from ancestor to ancestor. Betty says, and from directly utter birth until the age of fourteen she has been eating it up. You know—

stuff about Rob Roy and Walter Scott and Invérads Chiefs and Robin Hood and a lot of these reclusions before they invented economists, and I dipped into a lot of that stuff myself. It ain't reasonably like the pictures.

Being in love with Betty was no easy either you had got to be a Hero or you were practically the dirt under her feet. She had the notion maybe I have got

NORMAN ROCKWELL
SPRING TONIC
1936, oil on canvas
37" x 29", signed lower right
Saturday Evening Post, May 30, 1936 cover

Rockwell, as an avid fan of Mark Twain, was quite pleased to be awarded this important commission. It also satiated his omnipresent desire to travel and absorb local cultures, this time in Twain's hometown, Hannibal, Missouri. He completed the artwork for a deluxe book edition, widely beloved thereafter. *A World Book Encyclopedia* article described Rockwell's images of Mark Twain's folks as "the people who live in everybody's home town, barefoot teenage boys in particular." Rockwell later recreated his earlier Mark Twain book illustration for the cover of the *Post*, albeit making slight changes, perhaps for copyright reasons. The cover shows Aunt Polly giving Tom Sawyer his tonic, whilst the befuddled cat looks at the young hero. The composition clearly influenced his later painting for Brown & Bigelow Calendars, *Tender Years – Treating a Cold*, (1957, p. 137). An elderly couple is portrayed in a near identical pose as that of Aunt Polly and Tom in *Spring Tonic*, down to the patch-work blanket.

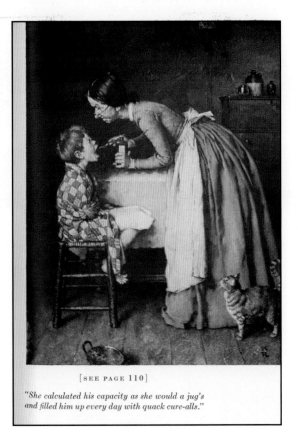

[SEE PAGE 110]

"She calculated his capacity as she would a jug's and filled him up every day with quack cure-alls."

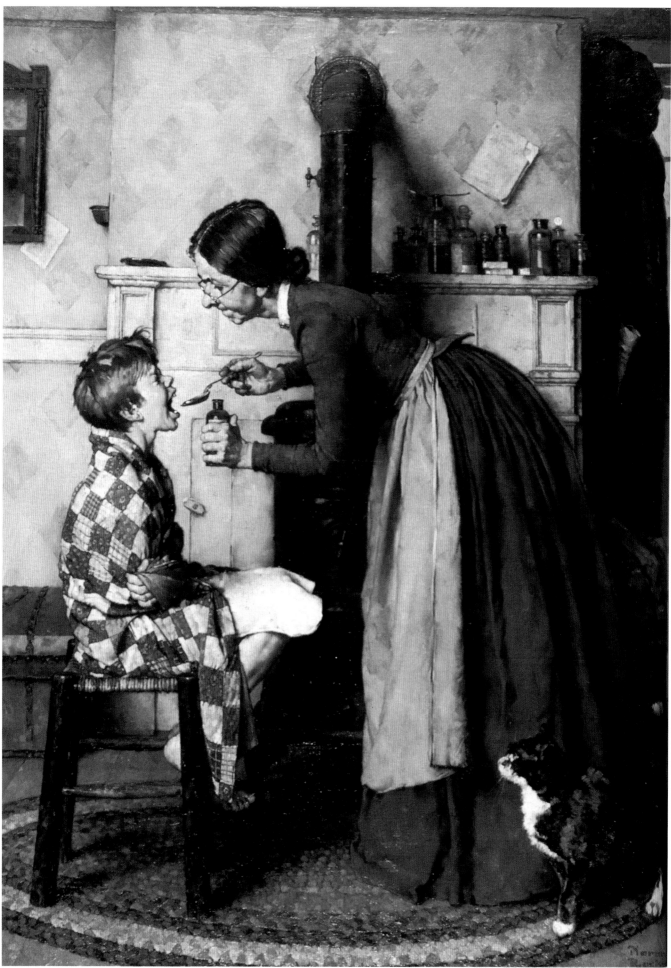

NORMAN ROCKWELL
LOVE OUANGA
1936, oil on canvas
30" x 62", signed lower right
American Magazine, June 1936, p. 56-57
Love Ouanga by Kenneth Perkins
'Spice slumped on a bench. The Blood of the Lamb
congregation gaped and wondered. A city gal
sho'nuff-what did she want with them?'

This politically charged painting is uncharacteristically Rockwell because he depicts African-Americans and uses the entire canvas for the composition, as compared with his smaller cover illustrations. The focal points are at each end of the painting: a young African-American girl interrupted in her prayers by an intruder's presence and the intruder, the well-dressed, light-skinned, "high yeller" woman cowers at the edge of her seat. *Love Ouanga* dealt with issues of family honor and voodoo practices in the deep South. 'Spice,' the intruding woman shown on the right, has her illegitimate son taken from her by one Aesop Barley, an influential local man. Spice turns to voodoo practices quite common in New Orleans to scare Aesop, the 'Big Boss,' to return her son. In the end, Spice succeeds in winning back her child and marries Aesop's son Tad Barley, who had always been Spice's true love. Rockwell chose the moment Spice enters the congregation to entice the viewer to read on. The socioeconomic implications of this painting were startling and quite daring for any magazine during the racially charged and notoriously intolerant 1930s, yet Rockwell took hold of such provocative content, and created a masterpiece.

Love OUANGA

*Spice's heart was singing with happiness when she answered the bell—
but she opened the door to trouble*

By Kenneth Perkins

SPICE MACKSON'S shotgun flat was sandwiched between a pool parlor and a warehouse used for storing Mexican and Southern wool. It was a happy flat, because of the gilt joss, the canaries, the baby, and the phonograph. Ceaselessly the latter ground out New York jazz until Cuban rumba records converted Spice to the truer African rhythms. To thestfible was forever dancing.

Light yellow of skin, so light that the stain of cigarettes showed on her slender finger, Spice humanized with the background she had created for herself. The yellow and mimmic tandrim suited to emanate from her. She favored mantel ornaments that were of cretmie, and although they were speckled secondhand things, they were gay and cheer-ful, and they increased the glow of the room.

When Spice had company, which was often, she put her baby to bed in the kitchen, on a mattress of Spanish moss spread over two packing cases. Spice then would paint her lion face, head her already tank growth of eyelashes, turn on the rumba muted with a dish towel, light an incense stick in the joss—and she was ready for her caller.

At night this would be some young man or other to take her to a dance. During the day it would be some woman,

Spice slumped on a bench. The Blood of the Lamb Congregation gaped and wondered. A city gal sho' nuff—what did she want with them?

perhaps, for a hair treatment. But, young or old, man or woman, she warmed to them all. People and things had the effect of starting silent harmonies in her. Her bones thrilled in a perpetual rhythm with the world. She loved her canary birds. She loved the overroad, its chickens, its smell of love and oleander and wine barrels, its smell of moss-muddy flagstone. She loved, above all things else, that little one, born without crutch pain, born a mogit, shining black brighter than a crow's wing in the sun. He was the whole world and all its fragrances, pleasant or pungent, rolled into one.

Now Spice was waving her hands in the air to dry the blood-red enamel she had painted on her blue nails. The harmony of sound and movement attracted the baby boy. Doubtless he felt it in

NORMAN ROCKWELL
THE TICKET SELLER - STUDY
1937, charcoal on paper
27 3/4" x 21 1/4", unsigned
Saturday Evening Post, April 24, 1937 cover

Norman Rockwell was exceptional at capturing the moods and ironies in everyday life. *The Ticket Seller* illustrates a man bored with his job, which incidentally helps so many others escape their tiresome lives. All around him are signs for exotic places and peaceful getaways, yet the ticket seller always remains behind. His expression is rather wistful as he peers out from the darkness of the ticket booth, which Rockwell has cleverly made appear as a jail cell.

Rockwell's study for *The Ticket Seller*, 1937, oil on board, 14" x 12"

NORMAN ROCKWELL
THE SPORT (MAN FISHING IN BOAT) - STUDY
1939, oil on board
13 3/4" x 10 3/4"
Saturday Evening Post, April 29, 1939 cover

To expedite the process of creating his iconic images, Rockwell developed a meticulous 7-step process. One crucial step in this process was to create 'color studies.' These were small works, usually about the size at which it might be reproduced in a magazine or book. He experimented with different colors for possible use in the final painting. This allowed him to see how they would appear to a reader when viewing the cover of a magazine on a newsstand.

This particular color study is very similar to the final painting, with few subtle changes such as the word "SPORT" in a different color, the position of the flies in his hat, and the lack of the can of worms in his bucket. Rough studies such as this are often left unsigned, as they were only used as a preparatory step en route to the final work.

NORMAN ROCKWELL
*WILLIE GILLIS - WHAT TO DO IN A BLACKOUT
- STUDY*
1942, charcoal on paper
28" x 23 3/4", signed and inscribed lower right
Saturday Evening Post, June 27, 1942 cover

NORMAN ROCKWELL
WILLIE GILLIS IN CHURCH - STUDY
1942, charcoal on paper
33" x 26 1/2", signed lower center "To Joe Busciglio, Best
of Luck, Norman Rockwell"
Saturday Evening Post, July 25, 1942 cover

The most representative of Rockwell's war covers are the Willie Gillis series. There are eleven images-the first appearing on October 4, 1941 and the last on October 5, 1946. Rockwell has said that this series grew out of his interest in "the plight of an inoffensive, ordinary little guy thrown into the chaos of war. He was not to be an avid, brave, blood-and–guts soldier, though a perfectly willing–if somewhat ineffective one."   At a square dance in Arlington, Rockwell discovered Robert Buck, whom he thought would make an ideal model. Buck, unfit for military duty, perfectly suited Rockwell's purposes. After the first several covers had been painted, Buck patriotically enlisted in the Naval Air Service. Rockwell cleverly completed the series by using photographs of Robert Buck in various settings until he came home from the War. Willie Gillis is an early prototype of the American anti-hero who has appeared so frequently in postwar literature and movies. Rockwell painted these covers at a time when citizens were expected to subjugate individuality and make a selfless contribution to the common cause. Willie Gillis contributes to the common cause, but nevertheless remains very much an individual.

NORMAN ROCKWELL
WILLIE GILLIS - CAT'S CRADLE
1943, oil on canvas
39" x 29", signed lower right
Saturday Evening Post, June 26 1943 cover

Cat's Cradle depicts Rockwell's WWII 'hero', Willie Gillis, playing the children's game Cat's Cradle with an Indian snake charmer. Clearly the boyish GI has pulled the wool over the eyes of the dumbfounded snake charmer, whose existence is dependent upon "snake charming" innocent tourists.

NORMAN ROCKWELL
***WINCHESTER STAGE COACH - HOW TO SOLVE YOUR CHRISTMAS
SHOPPING PROBLEM IN FIVE MINUTES***
1941, oil on canvas
31" x 66", signed lower right
Reader's Digest Christmas gift subscription advertisement, 1941

Rockwell's 1941 *Reader's Digest* Christmas gift subscription advertisement
depicts Dickens-like characters in 19th century English garb in this Winchester
Stage Coach scene jammed with people and carriage traffic. He illustrated
two Christmas gift subscription ads for *Reader's Digest* during his career. The
excitement and bustle of the Christmas season is accurately portrayed in this
crowded canvas of animated townsfolk.

Dolores Costello

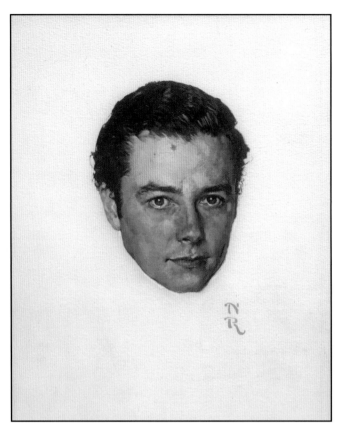

Tim Holt

Anne Baxter

Rockwell's ability to capture the likeness of an individual led to commissions for movie posters and playbills where he was given the opportunity to paint portraits of movie stars. In 1942, selected by film director Orson Welles and hired by RKO pictures, Rockwell created the movie poster for *The Magnificent Ambersons*, based on the novel by Booth Tarkington. Rockwell painted all six of the headlining star actors in the movie to Welles' delight: Anne Baxter, Richard Bennett, Dolores Costello, Joseph Cotton, Tim Holt, and Agnes Moorehead. The poster appeared on billboards and in several magazines. The movie was nominated for four Academy Awards including Best Picture and is considered one of Orson Welles' greatest masterpieces and by some critics, one of the ten best films of all time.

NORMAN ROCKWELL
THE MAGNIFICENT AMBERSONS
1942, oil on board
15 1/2" x 11 1/2", initialed lower right (each)
The Magnificent Ambersons movie poster, 1942

Agnes Moorehead

Joseph Cotton

Richard Bennett

NORMAN ROCKWELL
*SAMSON TEARING DOWN THE TEMPLE -
PORTRAIT OF VICTOR MATURE*
1949, oil on canvas
67" x 49 1/4", signed lower left
Entered in a competition sponsored by Famous
Artists School for a movie poster for Cecil B.
DeMille's *Samson and Delilah*

Norman Rockwell created this powerful, large-scale version of Samson in chains tearing down the temple for the film, *Samson and Delilah* directed by Cecil B. DeMille. Rockwell illustrated the final moment of the movie when Samson, having been blessed by God with extraordinary strength, begins to destroy the temple's pillars. He used dark colors and painterly brush strokes to illustrate the power of Samson and the heightened drama of this climactic moment. A strong image was needed to entice Americans to go to movie theaters. The Famous Artists School displayed the paintings entered in a movie poster competition at Macy's and other popular department stores. The competition was used to promote the movie and the Famous Artists School's art scholarship. A portrait of Rockwell painting the Samson movie poster was also used as an advertisement to enroll students in the Famous Artists School, a correspondence art class (see above).

The late J. Carter Brown, Director Emeritus of the National Gallery of Art in Washington D.C., commented upon first viewing this painting at the NMAI, *"it looks as if it naturally grew out of this marvelous paneling and its surrounding moldings. No one will ever believe that it is one of my favorite paintings, and that it is by Norman Rockwell, and hangs so perfectly in a Gilded Age Newport mansion."*

Above:
Photograph of Rockwell painting *Samson* used in an advertisement for the Famous Artists School

Left:
Actor Victor Mature posing for Rockwell as Samson on orange crates

While it would be ridiculous to make too close a formal comparison between these two works, which have very little in common apart from a general baroque feel, one genuine, one assumed, there is, I think, a point to be made. Van Dyck's great early canvas is a development of a composition famously tackled by his mentor, Rubens (in the National Gallery, London). With the supreme self-confidence of the brilliant twenty-year-old, Van Dyck set out to improve his master's work. Rubens' *Samson & Delilah* is brooding, contemplative, melancholy… Delilah seems drained of energy, sad but resigned about her betrayal. Van Dyck preferred the action version. His painting cranks up the tension, and makes the viewer hold his/her breath, making much of the fact that Samson might wake up at any moment. Here Delilah is an active participator, urgently hushing the hulking soldier wielding the shears and gingerly pulling back her brocade to allow access to Samson's hair. In a word, Van Dyck's approach is more cinematic, before cinema existed.

Of course, in Rockwell's case, being cinematic was in one sense the whole point. His image of the movie star Victor Mature in the role of Samson shows the climax of the story, and the film – as, with hair having grown back, he regains his strength and brings the temple down round the ears of the Philistines. The image's function was as a poster image – a means of attracting the public to the big film. In a kind of inversion of the process that Van Dyck achieved, Rockwell subsumes his more recognizable style in what is effectively a parody of High Baroque. Comparison with the photo on which the image is based confirms his intention. He is in fact making the image less cinematic, and by doing so he is gilding this most populist of art forms with the mantle of *high art*.

Ian A C Dejardin

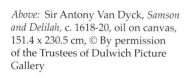

Above: Sir Antony Van Dyck, *Samson and Delilah,* c. 1618-20, oil on canvas, 151.4 x 230.5 cm, © By permission of the Trustees of Dulwich Picture Gallery

Right: Details from Norman Rockwell's *Samson Tearing Down the Temple*

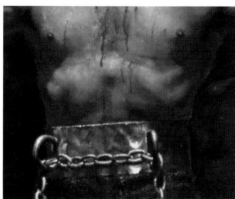

NORMAN ROCKWELL
MISS LIBERTY
1943, oil on canvas
41 3/4" x 31 1/4", signed lower right
Saturday Evening Post, September 4, 1943 cover

For seventy years, Rockwell painted nostalgic renditions of life in America. The ideas behind his imagery generally involved American values of family and community often sprinkled with irony. In *Miss Liberty*, the 1943 Labor Day cover, the artist took a giant step by creating a cultural icon for America, while symbolizing America itself. *Miss Liberty* represents women of the 1940s who went to work for the first time taking over men's jobs while they fought overseas. Women suddenly fulfilled roles to which they never aspired, nor even envisaged before: janitors, riveters, heavy equipment operators, mechanics, steel erectors. In short, *Miss Liberty* is emblematic of her times and the liberation of women in the workplace. Rockwell's *Rosie the Riveter* painted 3 months earlier, gained greater recognition than *Miss Liberty*; while similar conceptually, they are very different images that hold similar messages. The subtlety of the message and more painterly qualities demonstrated here are often compared to *Rosie,* his exaggerated image of a masculine, female riveter holding a rivet tool and a sandwich (page 188).

The *Saturday Evening Post* listed a number of occupations which were represented in *Miss Liberty*: gas station attendant, switchboard operator, grocery clerk, milkwoman, electrician, plumber, garage mechanic, stenographer, editor, reporter, baggage clerk, bus driver, railroad conductor, taxi driver, mechanical equipment maintenance person, truck driver, bookkeeper, farm worker, teacher, and public health worker. The *Post* invited its readers to notify them of other occupations they could find hidden therein. Rockwell later noted "getting the props all together and arranging them on the model had presented quite a problem," perhaps the hardest part of creating an artwork for this master artist/illustrator.

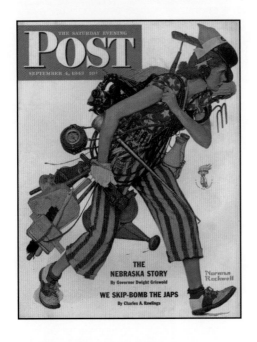

Far Left:
Saturday Evening Post cover,
September 4, 1943

Near Left:
Detail of emblem printed on
Miss Liberty Post cover

Norman Rockwell

NORMAN ROCKWELL
FREEDOM OF SPEECH - Poster
1943, original poster
30" x 21 1/2", US Government Printing Office

Rockwell created the *Four Freedoms* as a means to raise money for the war effort. These four works travelled to sixteen different cities and were able to raise $132 million for the war effort. The paintings produced by Rockwell were initially inspired by a speech presented by President Franklin D. Roosevelt in 1941, where he lists the four freedoms that every person must have, "everywhere in the world." These works are amongst Norman Rockwell's best in terms of both skillfulness and popularity.

President Franklin D. Roosevelt's Address to Congress, January 6, 1941 began:

"In the future days, which we seek to make secure, we look forward to a world founded upon four essential human freedoms:

The first is freedom of speech and expression - everywhere in the world."

 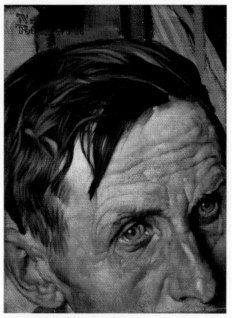

Above Left: Rockwell's *Freedom of Speech-Study*, 1942, oil on board, 21 1/2" x 16 1/2"

Above Right: Rockwell's *Freedom of Speech-Fragment of a Man's Head-Study*, 1942, oil on canvas, 12 1/2" x 10"

SAVE FREEDOM OF SPEECH

BUY WAR BONDS

NORMAN ROCKWELL
FREEDOM OF WORSHIP - *Poster*
1943, original poster
30" x 21 1/2", US Government Printing Office

"The second is freedom of every person to worship God in his own way - everywhere in the world."

Rockwell's *Freedom of Worship-Study*, 1942, oil and pencil on board, 20" x 18"

NORMAN ROCKWELL
FREEDOM FROM WANT - Poster
1943, original poster
30" x 21 1/2", US Government Printing Office

"The third is freedom from want - which, translated into world terms, means economic understandings which will secure to every nation a healthy peacetime life for its inhabitants - everywhere in the world."

OURS...to fight for

FREEDOM FROM WANT

NORMAN ROCKWELL
FREEDOM FROM FEAR - *Poster*
1943, original poster
30" x 21 1/2", US Government Printing Office

"The fourth is freedom from fear - which, translated into world terms, means a world-wide reduction of armaments to such a point and in such a thorough fashion that no nation will be in a position to commit an act of physical aggression against any neighbor- anywhere in the world.

That is no vision of a distant millennium. It is a definite basis for a kind of world attainable in our own time and generation. That kind of world is the very antithesis of the so-called new order of tyranny which the dictators seek to create with the crash of a bomb."

OURS...to fight for

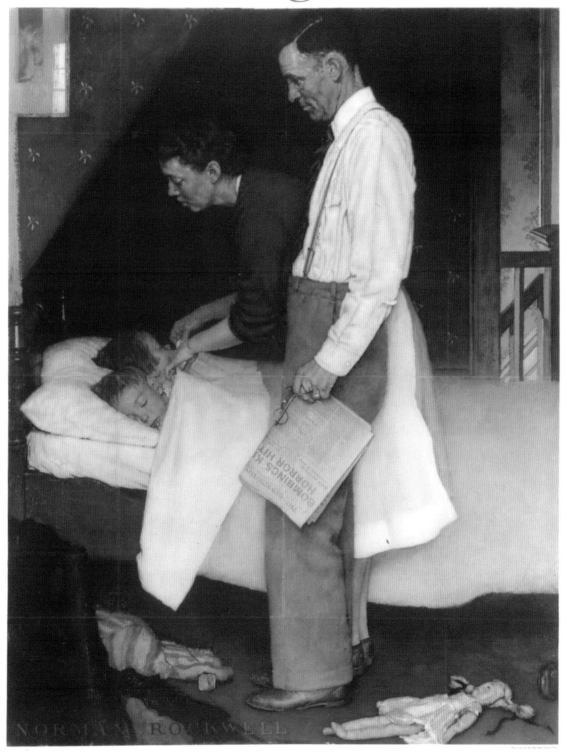

FREEDOM FROM FEAR

NORMAN ROCKWELL
DISABLED VETERAN - SOLDIER WITH US WAR BOND
1944, oil on canvas
43" x 34", signed lower right
Saturday Evening Post, July 1, 1944 cover

Rockwell's technique of placing a static figure in front of an action scene in this painting won him first prize from the Art Directors' contest in 1944. He later commented that he attributed this technique to the Old Masters. It gave life to an otherwise static setting. His somber palette added gravitas to the nature of war. The front figure holds the focus of the viewer and displays the ultimate reality of being wounded and returning home disabled. Rockwell used his Arlington neighbor, Roy Cole, who actually served in the 1st infantry division (the oldest division in the US Army) and returned home wounded. His name and Arlington address are visible on the war bond.

Disabled Veteran was reproduced as a *Saturday Evening Post* cover on July 1, 1944 as a tribute to the US soldier for his patriotism and sacrifices. It was a plaudit to Government, which cared for its wounded and fallen, with income from war bonds.

NORMAN ROCKWELL
NORMAN ROCKWELL VISITS A RATION BOARD
1944, oil on board
13 1/2" x 23 1/2", signed lower right
Saturday Evening Post, July 15, 1944
'Norman Rockwell Visits a Ration Board' p. 22-23

"I visited the Ration Board at Manchester, Vermont, to gather the subject matter for this painting, which appeared as a spread in the Saturday Evening Post. It was an interesting job, for ration boards were then an active factor in the American scene—something which directly or indirectly played a part in the life of everyone of us. I couldn't resist working myself into the painting—there I am at the extreme left. In addition to this painting, I did many small figures (see opposite right)—a parade of them which accompanied the painting as reproduced in the Post. The longer I observed such boards in action the more I felt like saying, 'Hats off!' to such workers the country over." –Norman Rockwell[1]

Norman Rockwell was one of the many artists to partake in the effort to document WWII. While short-lived, the Ration Board regulated and allocated the purchases of foodstuffs such as flour and sugar, as well as gasoline and other items of necessity. Only small amounts of these items in short supply could be purchased in order to conserve resources, and be fair to all. The controls Government imposed were exercised through coupon books and ration coins – a new currency minted solely for this purpose.

[1] Guptill, Arthur L. *Norman Rockwell, Illustrator.* New York: Watson-Guptill, 1946, page 88-89.

NORMAN ROCKWELL
YOU'LL MARRY ME AT NOON
1945, oil on canvas
45" x 32", signed lower left
'You'll Marry Me at Noon' by Vina Delmar
Ladies' Home Journal, January 1945, p. 24-25
'Tonight... the night before her wedding... she had met the only man
she had ever wanted to marry.'

This illustration for the story *'You'll Marry Me At Noon'* was published in the
Ladies' Home Journal, the first women's magazine in the US. It is a sleeker,
more stylish composition than Rockwell's earlier *Saturday Evening Post* covers
from the 1920's and 1930's, perhaps his best known works. Rockwell made
an artistic decision to switch to a flatter, more elegant composition much like
his contemporaries painted in the late 40's, 50's and 60's. The purpose of this
painting is to intrigue and, therefore invite the viewer to read the story. It
does not tell the story, but instead causes the observer to ask questions. When
Rockwell completed the painting, the art editor made the decision to focus
close-up on the woman and to crop out the man standing behind the woman
to make the story image more provocative. The image below shows the edited
and published use of the painting while on the right is the image as painted.

NORMAN ROCKWELL
CHARWOMEN IN THEATER - STUDY
1946, oil paint over photographic base
14 1/2" x 11", Signed "Norman Rockwell" bottom
right, inscribed "To Morgan Harding sincerely
Norman Rockwell" on the mat
Saturday Evening Post, April 6, 1946 cover

"This color study was painted directly upon a photographic print of my charcoal layout... the print having been purposely made at the actual size of a Post cover. Compare this study with the final painting... which was based on it. Often I make several of these color studies. Thus, having done my thinking in advance while working at relatively small scale, the actual cover painting can be accomplished very rapidly." -Norman Rockwell[1]

"It just came to me. I think I have always wanted to paint a charwoman or some similar type of worker – the poor little drudge who has to tidy up after more fortunate people have had a good time... Having decided on this charwomen subject and that the theatre is a logical setting, I made my little idea sketch. I decided to go to an actual theatre to obtain authentic information on such things as seats and aisles... I went to the office of the Shubert Theatres in New York... The Physical Properties Manager felt that the Majestic Theatre, where Carousel was playing, was typical, so we decided on that. A minor hitch came when I learned that just to turn on the lights would cost about forty dollars... After considerable negotiation, a way was found to reduce this force to one electrician and his assistant. With this adjusted, off we went to the Majestic, where I sketched and measured while a photographer took some pictures – one never knows how much information he may need when he gets to work far from his original source... Then back I hurried to Arlington where two neighbors, Mrs. Harvey McKee and Mrs. Charles Crofut, posed as the charwomen. I felt hesitant about asking them to represent such humble characters, but they were very good sports about it." – Norman Rockwell[1]

[1] Guptill, Arthur L. *Norman Rockwell, Illustrator*. New York: Watson-Guptill, 1946, p. 52-53

NORMAN ROCKWELL
APRIL FOOLS -
GIRL WITH SHOPKEEPER
1948, oil on canvas
18" x 17", signed lower center right
Saturday Evening Post, April 3, 1948 cover

This work was one of only three April Fools covers Rockwell painted for the *Saturday Evening Post.* In this image, a young girl has entered an antique shop and is talking to the shopkeeper amid various oddities. The scene contains nearly sixty jokes which Rockwell devised for the reader to discover. Some are easily spotted at once, such as Rockwell's signature written backwards and spelled incorrectly; while others are much more difficult to find, such as the portrait of Abraham Lincoln in a Confederate uniform. This cover remains one of the most popular from his *Saturday Evening Post* oeuvre because it exhibits Rockwell's wonderful sense of humor as well as his masterful artistic talent and attention to detail. The Old Masters are heralded by Rockwell including the iconic *Mona Lisa* with a halo, as another April Fool conundrum to discover.

Note: The sculpture in the painting's lower right corner represents an unlikely combination of two of sculptor John Rogers' most popular Victorian works, *Wounded to the Rear* (below, left) and *Coming to the Parsonage* (below, right).

Wounded to the Rear   *Coming to the Parsonage*

April Fools Jokes

1. Cupboard has two kinds of molding
2. Insignia is on the back of fireman's helmet
3. A North American pileated Woodpecker's head on a crane's body
4. Green and red lights are reversed on the ship's lantern
5. Electric bulbs growing on the plant
6. Head of the little girl on a man's bust
7. Penholder has a pencil eraser
8. A rat's tail on the chipmunk
9. Two different seasons are shown through the two windows
10. Book's titles are vertical, not horizontal
11. No shelf under the books
12. Goat's head and a deer's antlers
13. Top of the brass vase is suspended
14. Antique dealer's head appears on the dolls
15. Antique dealer has lace on his right shirt cuff
16. Potted plant is atop the lit stove
17. Sea gull has crane's legs
18. There is a horse saddle on the goat with deer antlers
19. *Mona Lisa* has a halo
20. *Mona Lisa* is facing the wrong way
21. The stove says 'April Fool' on it
22. Abraham Lincoln is wearing General Grant's military coat
23. Antique dealer's shoe has a spur on it
24. Brass kettle has two spouts
25. Stove is missing a leg
26. Mouse and ground mole are conferring
27. The ground mole's tracks are through the wooden floor
28. Two different kinds of floor in the shop - wooden planks and tiles
29. Girl's shoes do not match
30. Norman Rockwell's signature is reversed
31. Norman Rockwell's signature is spelled wrong
32. Flowers growing out of the floor
33. The ball fringe is standing straight up
34. Dog's head on a cat's body
35. Racoon's tail on a cat's body
36. This statue is a combination of two John Rogers' statues: the soldier from *Wounded to the Rear* and the woman from *Coming to the Parsonage* (statues on page 118)
37. Girl's socks do not match
38. Doll has hooves instead of feet
39. Small girl on the shelf is not sitting on anything
40. Gun barrel is in the wrong place
41. Small girl on the shelf is holding a skunk
42. Girl's purse is a book
43. Only half a strap on the girl's purse
44. Girl has five fingers and a thumb on her left hand
45. Girl's sweater is buttoned incorrectly
46. There are nine branches on the traditionally seven branched candelabra
47. Girl's hair is down on one half and braided on the other
48. Phone has two mouthpieces
49. Phone is not connected to anything
50. Antique dealer's face is in the clock
51. A beast is crouched on the upper shelf
52. There is a candle where a kerosene lamp should be
53. The sampler with American Flags is dated 1216 (first American Flag was in 1776)
54. Coffeepot's spout is upside down
55. Tea cup is not hanging by the handle
56. Barbed wire, not clothesline

NORMAN ROCKWELL
***BREAKFAST TABLE POLITICAL ARGUMENT -
OIL STUDY***
1948, oil on acetate on board
10 1/4" x 11", signed lower right and inscribed,
"To Herb Herrick, Sincerely, Norman Rockwell"
Saturday Evening Post, October 30, 1948

The 1948 Presidential Election marked a turning point for the Republican
Party as the Democratic Party seemed weak and unstable. This painting
reflects the historic battle of Thomas Dewey (R) versus Harry Truman (D)
for President of the United States. The husband, dressed for work, shouts
fiercely at his wife who pouts stubbornly with folded arms. The husband
points sharply at a magazine cover showing his support for Dewey, while his
wife clearly supports Truman. Both are so involved in the debate over their
candidates that neither seems to pay any attention to the upset child at their
feet nor to the hungry dog in the corner. *Breakfast Table Political Argument*
is both witty and charming in depicting a suburban American lifestyle. It
is a classic example of Rockwell's traditionally entertaining approach to the
world and to his cover art.

Rockwell's pencil study for *Breakfast Table Political Argument*
1948, pencil on paper, 31" x 34"

NORMAN ROCKWELL
BRIDGE GAME - THE BID
1948, oil on canvas
46 1/2" x 38 1/2", signed lower left
Saturday Evening Post, May 15, 1948 cover

The composition for *Bridge Game* was particularly challenging and an unlikely pose for it is a one-point perspective, aerial view. Each card player's hand is simultaneously exposed for the benefit of bridge-playing aficionados amongst the *Post* readership. Rockwell knew nothing about the game and required the help of a bridge game expert and a wooden plank in order to undertake this work. The long plank was nailed to the balcony floor of his photographer's studio over a table posed with four models. Each model held cards carefully arranged by 'Red,' Rockwell's locally (Chicago) selected bridge expert to complete the scene. The artist then asked the photographer to venture out to the plank's edge to take a bird's-eye shot 'straight down' for his use in creating the cover image. The exposure of all card players' hands at once, as if from a secret casino security room above the players, was Rockwell's notion, albeit before such observation rooms existed.

NORMAN ROCKWELL
SEASON'S GREETINGS
1949, tempera on board
11" x 22", signed lower right
Ford Motor Company advertisement

Season's Greetings is a Ford Motor Company Christmas advertisement. It juxtaposes a horse drawn sled with a Model T Ford as they travel past each other; a marked difference in travel options. The excited dogs and scattered presents coupled with the expressions of the characters deliver the merits of a Ford along with the convivial message of 'Season's Greetings.'

S

NORMAN ROCKWELL
SHUFFLETON'S BARBERSHOP - STUDY
1950, oil on canvas
33" x 31", unsigned
Saturday Evening Post, April 29, 1950 cover

This study is an example of Norman Rockwell's devotion and commitment to every aspect of creating a *Saturday Evening Post* cover. This nearly monochromatic study presented many challenges; the most difficult was painting a poorly lit room as seen looking through a dark room. This work again exhibits his lifelong fascination with the Old Masters, in this case, Vermeer. The artist worked steadily over a three-month period with gloomy weather, each day cloudier than before. Rockwell began to consider his work a failure until he finally found a way, during a break in the weather, to get the sharp contrasts he wanted to capture in the painting. He ultimately succeeded in getting exactly what he sought by creating a collage from his sketches and photos. His final efforts paid off and he created one of his most notable paintings. Depicting an after-hours moment, a few local men gather in an adjoining room to the barbershop to play music and relax after a long day. The main character, the protagonist, in this painting is the barbershop itself. A living entity of another kind, it heralds simple down home American music-making in a dormant setting.

Rockwell's *Shuffleton's Barbershop*
1950, oil on canvas, 46 1/4" x 43"

NORMAN ROCKWELL
SOLITAIRE
1950, oil on canvas
27" X 25", signed lower left
Saturday Evening Post, August 19, 1950 cover

During the 1950's, the public continued to steadily turn to *Post* covers as reflections of their American way of life. As the premier magazine cover artist and visionary of our national identity, Norman Rockwell was the perfect artist to depict prototypical American figures; to wit: the traveling salesman. For this cover, Rockwell sought to dispel the myth that all commercial travelers spent their nights with an icy brew and a 'hot' woman. Many readers wrote to the *Post* thanking them for his touching and honest portrayal of a lonely salesman. Rockwell went on to use the theme of the traveling salesman for a Brown & Bigelow Four Seasons calendar. From that series, there is another classic Rockwell image of the traveling salesman whereby he is selling an 'icebox' (refrigerator) to an Eskimo in the midst of an Alaskan Winter.

Rockwell's *Traveling Salesman-The Expert Salesman*
1964, oil wash on board, 15 1/2" x 15 1/2"

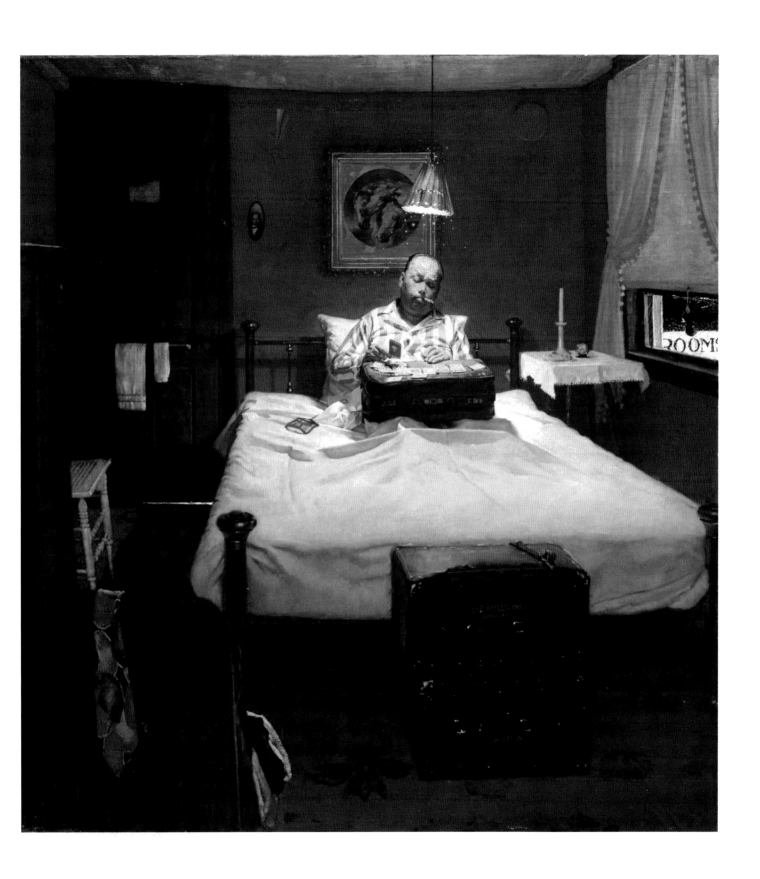

NORMAN ROCKWELL
A DAY IN THE LIFE OF A LITTLE GIRL-STUDY
1952, charcoal on paper
22 ¼" x 21 ¼", signed and inscribed lower right
Saturday Evening Post, August 30, 1952 cover

This charcoal study for *A Day in the Life of a Little Girl* shows a very expressive child going through her daily activities. Rockwell met his model, Mary Whelan, at a basketball game in which his son Tommy was playing. The artist later commented that she was "the best darn model I ever had, sad one minute, happy the next, and she raised her eyebrows just the right way…" Mary Whelan became Rockwell's favorite model and a very important figure in his paintings due to her charismatic, ever-changing face. In this painting her image appears twenty-one times, each with a different emotion and attitude; a compliment to the model, but more especially to the artist's abilities.

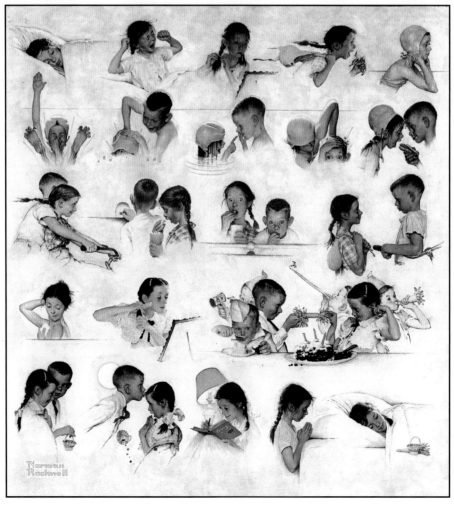

Rockwell's *A Day In The Life Of A Little Girl*
1952, oil on canvas, 45" x 42"

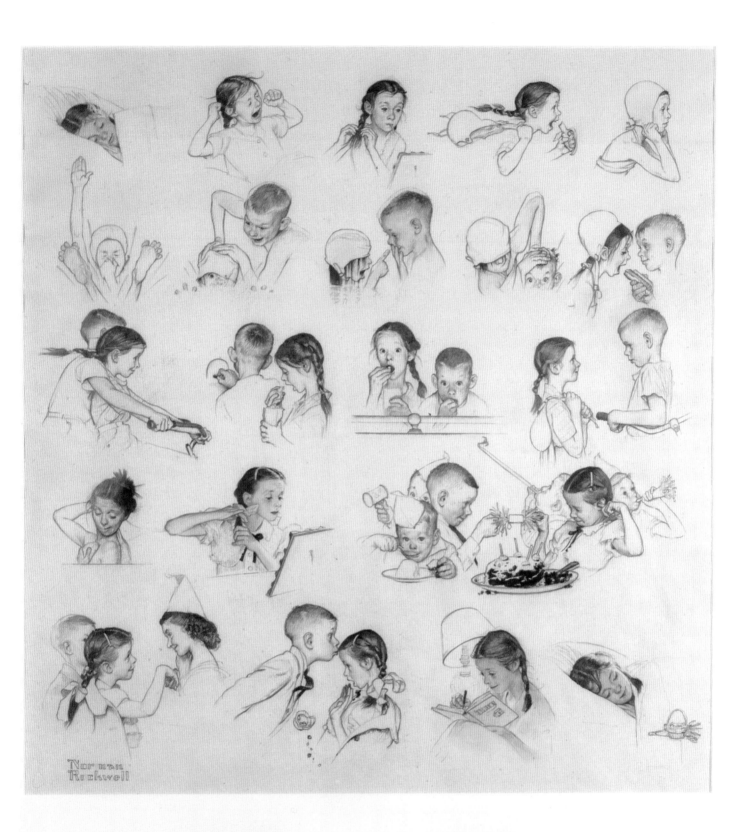

NORMAN ROCKWELL
CHOIR BOY COMBING HAIR FOR EASTER
1954, oil on canvas
29" x 26 1/2", signed lower right and inscribed
Saturday Evening Post, April 17, 1954 cover

During the 1950s, when more than half of Rockwell's forty-one *Post* covers featured children, he made numerous references to his own childhood in his paintings, this is illustrated particularly in *Choir Boy*. Recalling his days in the church choir, Rockwell wrote, "On Sundays in the choir room… The sexton, poking his head around the door, would yell that it was time for us to enter the church. Plastering down our cowlicks, pushing, jostling, we'd form two lines. Then, suddenly, we'd grow quiet and, solemn-faced, march into the church.[1]" Rockwell's painted version of this memory features a choir boy in hurried preparation for an Easter service. He uses a Gothic-like paneled archway to frame the setting and through it we glimpse the proof of last-minute preparations in the scattered clothing, sneakers, and abandoned roller skates. Such "behind-the-scenes" treatment appears frequently throughout Rockwell's *Post* covers, a vantage point which allowed him to show the human side of his protagonists with sensitivity and compassion.

[1.] *Norman Rockwell Album, The*. New York: Doubleday & Company, Inc., 1961, p. 140.

NORMAN ROCKWELL
TENDER YEARS - TREATING A COLD - STUDY
1957, pencil
15" x 15", signed lower right
Brown & Bigelow Four Seasons Calendar (Spring), 1957

NORMAN ROCKWELL
TENDER YEARS - TREATING A COLD
1957, oil and pencil
18" x 18", signed lower right

Rockwell created numerous calendar illustrations for Brown & Bigelow, the nation's largest and most prolific calendar printer and distributor. His calendars for Brown & Bigelow usually followed the same characters through the changing seasons of a year. Rockwell painted his "four seasons" theme for Brown & Bigelow for sixteen years, from 1948 to 1964. This example from the *Tender Years* series focuses on a long-married couple in their day-to-day lives, taking care of each other in a way that only a lifetime together can create.

Left: Rockwell's Summer image, *Tender Years-Mowing the Lawn*, 1957, oil on canvas, 18" x 18"

Right: Rockwell's Autumn image, *Tender Years-Moth Holes*, 1957, oil on canvas, 18" x 18"

NORMAN ROCKWELL
TWO CHILDREN PRAYING
1959, oil on canvas
13 1/4" x 32", signed lower left
Advertisement for General Outdoor Advertising Company
Originally appeared as a billboard advertisement over Union Square for
Longchamps Restaurant (see photo on opposite page)

A dark starry background is used in this nearly solemn, inspiring, contemporary Christmas billboard advertisement. Rockwell depicts a young boy and girl praying to one especially bright star set against the blackened sky. This simple scene evokes a 'holy night' ambience, alluding to the classic nativity scene with a lone bright star in the East. That lone star led the three Magi to baby Jesus in the biblical Christmas story.

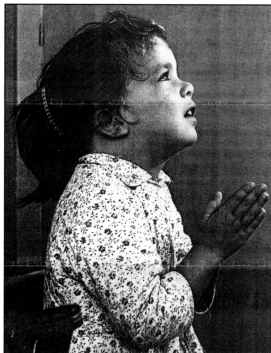

Photograph of Catharine B. Deeley

Longchamps Restaurant billboard over Union Square

NORMAN ROCKWELL
BOY GRADUATE
1959 , oil on canvas
74 1/2" x 36", signed lower right
Saturday Evening Post, June 6, 1959 cover

Norman Rockwell has perfectly captured the expression of a youthful college graduate with unabashed optimism, coupled with newfound bewilderment at the real world he faces. Rockwell separately provided a background for the finished cover which is comprised of newspaper headlines screaming contemporary problems to be shouldered by this young grad and his generation. The headlines ranged from Russia's "Khrushchev Warns West of War Danger" to "UN Atom Study Panel Sees Fall-Out Peril." "Inflation Number-One Problem," "State officials to Seek US Help for Job Woes," are all problems similarly faced by young graduates today, half a century later. Rockwell's son, Tom, posed for this near life-size portrait as the boy graduate. The *Post* added another contrast between its readers optimism symbolized by a graduation ceremony versus the realistic troubles facing the world in 1959, into which graduates entered. With this simple, but complex image, the magazine cover had now delved into the political realm.

Photographs of Tom (left) and Norman Rockwell (right) posing for *Boy Graduate*.
Rockwell, N. Photographs, Reference: *Boy Graduate*, 1960: Norman Rockwell Archival Collections, Norman Rockwell Museum, Stockbridge, MA.

NORMAN ROCKWELL
TRIPLE SELF-PORTRAIT - STUDY
1960, charcoal, gouache, and oil on board
13 1/2" x 10 1/2", signed and inscribed lower right
"My best to Jack Connors, sincerely, Norman Rockwell"
Saturday Evening Post, February 13, 1960 cover

Rockwell's *Triple Self-Portrait* (page 210) is one of the most famous self-portraits ever created. Artists inspired by Rockwell's creativity and wit have replicated and emulated this image many times over, in advertisements and in uncounted poster images as well as by amateur Sunday painters and copyists, with endless variations on his theme. This study concept was earmarked for use on the cover of the *Post*, which was intended to herald the launching of Rockwell's autobiography on February 13, 1960. The book was serialized in the *Post* over several issues. The study shows Rockwell's thought process leading up to the finished cover design. Around the self-portrait study is a virtual collage of the chapter headings in his book as published by Doubleday entitled, *My Adventures as an Illustrator*. It was released simultaneously with the *Post* magazine serialization.

Vignettes from Rockwell's chapter headings published in *My Adventures as an Illustrator* (*clockwise from top left*):

I. Scairt as a Rabbit, Bold as a Bear; II. I Sign My Name in Blood; III. I Meet the Body Beautiful; VI. Great Expectations; IX. The Mansion on Mount Tom Road; XII. The Deacon Goes Society; XVI. I Rise From the Ashes

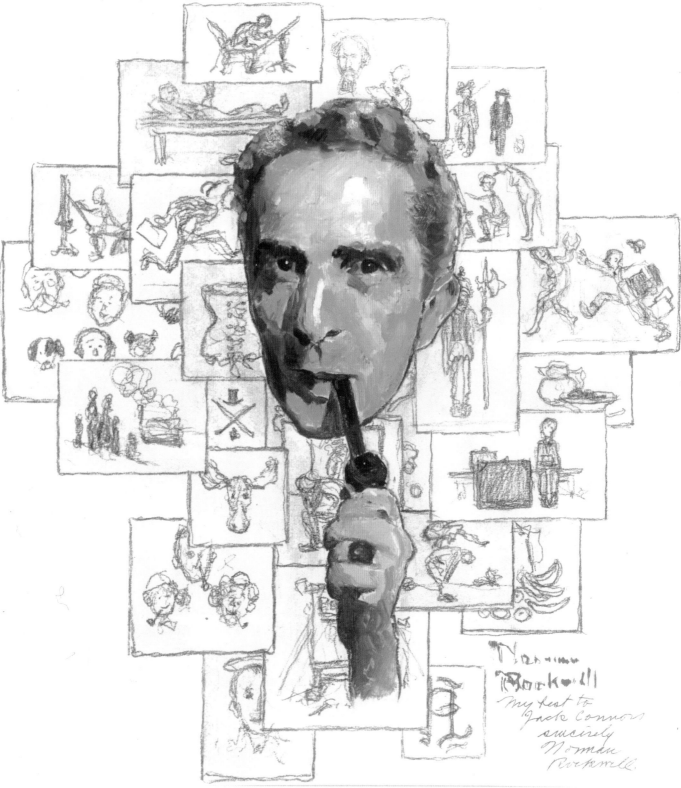

NORMAN ROCKWELL
LUNCH BREAK WITH KNIGHT
1962, oil on canvas
34" x 32", signed lower left
Saturday Evening Post, November 3, 1962 cover

Norman Rockwell conceived of this *Post* cover after visiting the Higgins Armory Museum in Worcester, MA, where he viewed one of the world's most extensive collections of armor. The austerity of the museum's Medieval Great Hall is playfully interrupted in this humorous scene. A horse directs its impossibly animated and censorious stare at the museum guard, who is relaxing 'taking a lunch break,' on the plinth. The guard treats the armor as an impromptu coat rack, remaining contentedly unaware of his audience. Light streaming in from the peaked Gothic windows acts as a spotlight on the guard's breach of museum decorum. This painting has a textured surface unlike any of his other works, perhaps an experiment.

Above Left: Norman Rockwell experimenting with 'texturizing' the surface varnish of *Lunch Break with Knight* with a broom, 1962

Above Right: Norman Rockwell posing for *Lunch Break with Knight* at the Higgins Armory Museum, Worcester, MA, 1962

Rockwell, N. Photographs, Reference: *Lunch Break with Knight,* 1962: Norman Rockwell Archival Collections, Norman Rockwell Museum, Stockbridge, MA.

NORMAN ROCKWELL
PORTRAIT OF NEHRU
1962, oil on canvas
17 3/4" x 20 1/2", signed and inscribed
lower right "New Delhi, India"
Saturday Evening Post, January 19, 1963 cover

In depicting Jawaharlal Nehru, the first Prime Minister of India who served from 1947 until 1964, Rockwell showed the powerful leader in a partial profile looking into the distance in deep thought. For the background, Rockwell chose to include a wallpaper-like pattern of Hindu figures praying and two symbols representing peace and war. In 1962, when this portrait was painted, Nehru had just won his last election and was facing turmoil with India's increasingly violent and aggressive neighbor, China. Rockwell depicts this crucial figure in India's history as an educated, intellectually enlightened man trying to decide what path is best for his country.

Jawaharlal Nehru posing for his portrait, India, 1962

AFTER THE *POST*
1964-1973

NORMAN ROCKWELL
THE PROBLEM WE ALL LIVE WITH - STUDY
1963, gouache on illustration board
13" x 21", signed lower right
Look magazine, January 14, 1964

Rockwell's *The Problem We All Live With,* first published in the January 14, 1964 issue of *Look* magazine, effectively depicts a significant moment in history as a young girl is marched into school by 'headless' government officials. His decision to crop the men at their shoulders brings more emphasis to the courageous child, Ruby Bridges, walking to her New Orleans elementary school on the first day of desegregation. In the first study (shown above), Rockwell depicted only two US Marshals in front of the little girl. However, as his idea developed, he added two more Marshals behind her, framing the central figure. Rockwell's socially aware image for *Look* had an untold effect on his audience. He depicted serious questions of societal change and in many ways awakened the nation to important issues of substance and debate. For the first time, he painted civil rights and human-interest images without his classically ironic, humorous subjects. It was the work of a 'new Rockwell,' hitherto unknown to his public. He had changed focus and in the process changed the way his audience thought-they morphed into a more liberal monolith and the strength of Rockwell's images affected his whole nation.

NORMAN ROCKWELL
***PEACE CORPS IN ETHIOPIA
(SCHOOLROOM) - STUDY***
1966, pencil and oil on illustration board
8" x 12 1/4", signed and inscribed lower right,
"sincerely, Norman Rockwell"
Look magazine story illustration, June 14, 1966

Peace Corps volunteer, John Schafer (neighbor of Rockwell in Arlington) teaches a secondary school class in this Peace Corps scene, an initial concept for a *Look* magazine commission. In the end, Rockwell did not use this study prepared in Debra Markos, Ethiopia, but used instead a portrayal of an Ethiopian farmer by his plow in Dessie, Ethiopia (shown below).

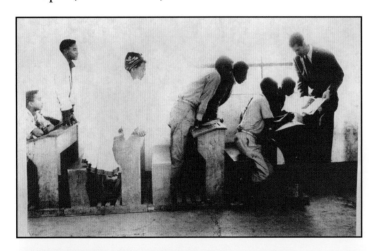

Top:
Photograph of John Schafer posing for *Schoolroom* study

Bottom:
Norman Rockwell's *Peace Corps in Ethiopia*, 1966, oil on canvas, 17" x 25"

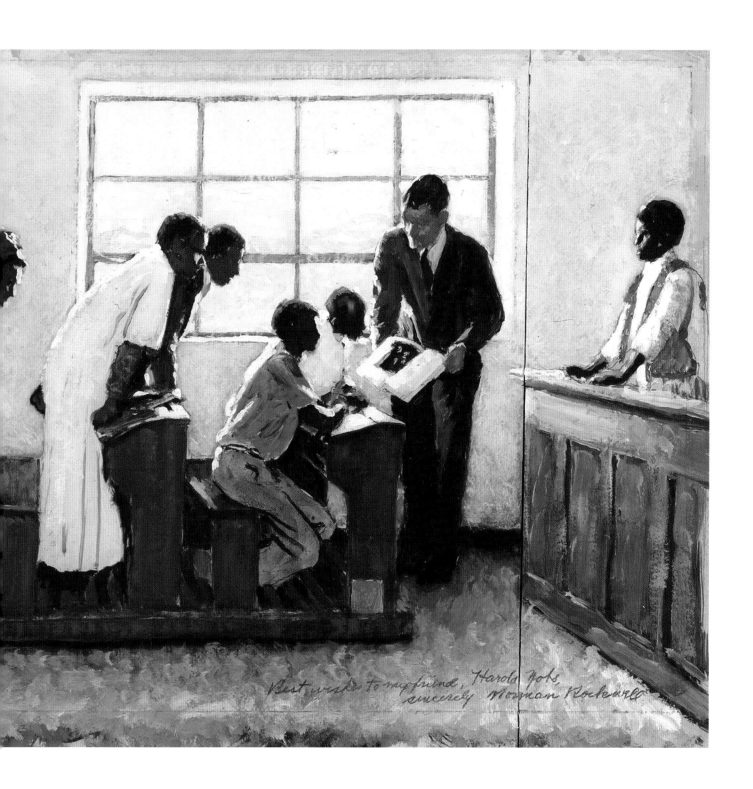

Best wishes to my friend, Harold Yoh,
sincerely Norman Rockwell

NORMAN ROCKWELL
RUSSIAN SCHOOLROOM - EDUCATION
1967, oil on canvas
15" X 37", signed lower right
Look magazine, 'Education' article, October 3, 1967, p. 48-49

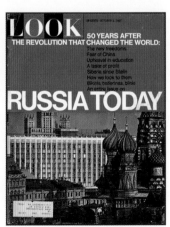

Rockwell's *Russian Schoolroom* depicts a classroom filled with students all facing the teacher and a bust of Vladimir Lenin, Russian revolutionary who led the Communist 'October Revolution' in 1917. The students have their textbooks open and are paying attention with one exception, a single student looking away. Rockwell's painting suggests that the boy is looking out the window to the future, perhaps to grow up to be like former USSR President Mikhail Gorbachev, a great reform leader who orchestrated the demise of the Communist Party. After six decades of humorous and satiric views of American life in the *Saturday Evening Post*, Rockwell finally began to create political statements. In his last decade, he sought assignments from *Look* which allowed him to travel more and create politically significant images as *Russian Schoolroom*, and other socially conscious works such as *The Problem We All Live With*. These were perhaps some of Rockwell's best works.

Photograph of Rockwell with Russian schoolchildren in the hallway, Moscow, Russia, 1967

Photograph of Rockwell with Russian schoolchildren in classroom, Moscow, Russia, 1967

Photograph of contemplative Russian schoolchildren, Moscow, Russia, 1967

Photograph of Rockwell working on a preliminary study for *Russian Schoolroom*, Italy, 1967

Rockwell, N. Photographs, Reference: *Russian Schoolroom* 1967: Norman Rockwell Archival Collections, Norman Rockwell Museum, Stockbridge, MA.

NORMAN ROCKWELL
THE RIGHT TO KNOW - STUDY
1968, oil on board
11 1/2" x 21 1/2", signed and inscribed lower right
"Sketch for 'Right to Know',/my love to Abigail
and/Dr. and Mrs. Maurice Bernstein/cordially
Norman Rockwell"

Look magazine, August 20, 1968, p. 48-49

"We are the governed, but we govern too. Assume our love of country, for it is only the simplest of self-love. Worry little about our strength, for we have our history to show for it. And because we are strong, there are others who have hope. But watch us more closely from now on, for those of us who stand here mean to watch those we put in the seats of power. And listen to us, you who lead, for we are listening harder for the truth that you have not always offered us. Your voice must be ours, and ours speaks of cities that are not safe, and of wars we do not want, of poor in a land of plenty, and of a world that will not take the shape our arms would give it. We are not fierce, and the truth will not frighten us. Trust us, for we have given you our trust. We are the governed, remember, but we govern too."

'*The Right to Know,' Look* magazine
August 20, 1968

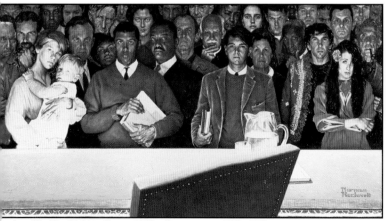

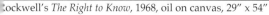

Rockwell's *The Right to Know*, 1968, oil on canvas, 29" x 54"

'The Right to Know,' *Look* magazine article, August 20, 1968

NORMAN ROCKWELL
FATHER'S RETURN HOME
1973, oil and graphite on canvas
40" x 35", signed lower right
American Mutual Insurance Company Christmas card

This illustration for an American Mutual Insurance Christmas card shows a classic Rockwellian, wholesome family at a time in Rockwell's career when the majority of his illustrations focused on world affairs and more serious concerns. Over the years, many visitors to the NMAI have commented on this particular image, usually noting that "today, even the family dog doesn't greet the father like that!" The technique of incorporating a circle of red, from the mother's dress to her shoes to the daughter's clothes up to the father's hat, against a flat background, similar to illustrator Al Parker, accentuates the focus on the all-American family (Mother, Father, Son, Daughter, Cat and Dog).

Above: Father's Return Home - Study, charcoal and graphite on paper, 39 3/4" x 34 3/4"

THE SATURDAY EVENING POST

WORLD WAR I AND AFTER
1916-1919

As Norman Rockwell was beginning his relationship with *The Saturday Evening Post (SEP)*, his covers focused primarily on children. The artist felt most comfortable illustrating simplistic scenes with children for they lent themselves to humorous escapades and ironic dilemmas to which everyone could relate. Such prototypical covers are seen in his very first *Post* commission, *The Baby Carriage* (May 20,1916; page 164) and then again on his second cover, *Circus Barker* (June 3, 1916; page 164). In *The Baby Carriage*, Billy Paine, his favorite boy model, posed as the unhappy sitter pushing the baby carriage while his friends get to play baseball. Billy died in a tragic accident when he was 13, but Rockwell had managed to pose him for fifteen covers, "…the best kid model I ever used." Rockwell's delightful images of children in wondrous settings were a welcome relief in a time of war and hardship. While other periodical illustrators focused on the horrors of World War I, he scarcely touched such subjects. In fact, Rockwell portrayed only two military images during these last few years of the decade and no action scenes. The military illustrations showed a sailor tenderly longing for his sweetheart (*Sailor Dreaming of Girlfriend*, January 18, 1919; page 165) (interestingly signed by the artist to reflect his own military service, "Norman Rockwell U.S.N.R.F."); and an Army hero proudly marching along in a makeshift impromptu parade of children (*The Doughboy and His Admirers*, February 22, 1919; page 43 and cover). During this period and until 1926, the covers were printed in duo-tone black and red, and Rockwell had to work with the constraints of *The Saturday Evening Post's* famous parallel bars masthead. The parameters within which Rockwell was forced to work never stifled his creativity.

May 20, 1916

June 3, 1916

August 5, 1916

September 16, 1916

October 14, 1916

December 9, 1916

January 13, 1917

May 12, 1917

June 16, 1917

FOLLOWING THE RED CROSS—By Elizabeth Frazer

October 27, 1917

Captain Schlotterwerz—By Booth Tarkington. England After the War—By Isaac F. Marcosson

January 26, 1918

All American—By Irvin S. Cobb

May 18, 1918

Gerald Stanley Lee—Edward N. Hurley—Wallace Irwin—Arthur Train
Sinclair Lewis—Neville Taylor Gherardi—Frederick Orin Bartlett

August 10, 1918

THE ZERO HOUR—By GEORGE PATTULLO

September 21, 1918

Edith Wharton—Octavus Roy Cohen—Peter Clark Macfarlane
Isaac F. Marcosson—Basil King—Albert W. Atwood—Rob Wagner

January 18, 1919

So This is Germany—By George Pattullo

February 22, 1919

George Randolph Chester—Samuel G. Blythe—May Edginton—Gerald Stanley Lee
Will Payne—Meyer Bloomfield—Henry Watterson—Nalbro Bartley—Wallace Irwin

March 22, 1919

MORE THAN TWO MILLION A WEEK

April 26, 1919

★ 165

June 14, 1919

June 28, 1919

August 9, 1919

September 6, 1919

September 20, 1919

October 4, 1919

December 20, 1919

THE SATURDAY EVENING POST

THE ROARING TWENTIES

(1920-1929)

The 'Roaring Twenties' was a time of celebration, a decade of bathtub gin coupled with social, cultural and artistic transformations. Americans had lost their innocence during WWI and afterwards experienced great societal upheaval, passing from old traditions to flashy new styles. Technological improvements offered radio broadcasting, talking movies, penicillin, jazz and a newfound romanticism encouraged by iconic Rudolph Valentino, Greta Garbo and 'Flappers' galore. During this decade, Rockwell visited Europe a half dozen times, observing how similar people were everyplace he traveled. The artist was determined to make that point to our diverse nation at home. He began to portray children in 'puppy love' (*Little Spooners*, April 24, 1926; page 174) and adults daydreaming with their thoughts floating above their heads (*Daydreaming Bookkeeper*, June 7, 1924; page 172), but always posed with universal expressions in familiar settings. His characters shared emotions and challenging moments with their audience. A perfect example is the bachelor trying to mend his socks in *Threading the Needle* (April 8, 1922; page 59). A common thread was expressed in this overarching illustration message. There was never a need for language or cultural translation in his works.

January 17, 1920

February 7, 1920

March 27, 1920

May 1, 1920

May 15, 1920

June 19, 1920

July 31, 1920

August 28, 1920

October 9, 1920

October 23, 1920

December 4, 1920

January 29, 1921

March 12, 1921

June 4, 1921

July 9, 1921

August 13, 1921

October 1, 1921

December 3, 1921

January 14, 1922

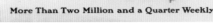

February 18, 1922

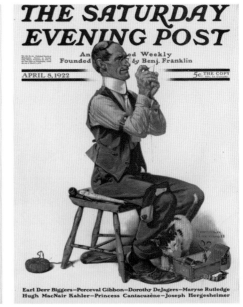

April 8, 1922

April 29, 1922

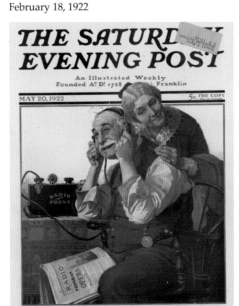

May 20, 1922

June 10, 1922

August 19, 1922

September 9, 1922

November 4, 1922

December 2, 1922

February 3, 1923

March 10, 1923

April 28, 1923

May 26, 1923

June 23, 1923

August 18, 1923

September 8, 1923

November 10, 1923

December 8, 1923

March 1, 1924

April 5, 1924

May 3, 1924

June 7, 1924

June 14, 1924

July 19, 1924

August 30, 1924

September 27, 1924

October 18, 1924

November 8, 1924

December 6, 1924

January 31, 1925

April 18, 1925

May 16, 1925

June 27, 1925

July 11, 1925

August 29, 1925

September 19, 1925

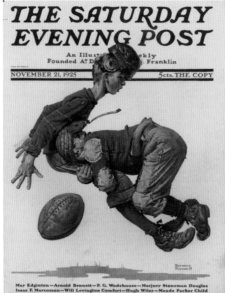

November 21, 1925

December 5, 1925

January 9, 1926

February 6, 1926

March 27, 1926

April 24, 1926

May 29, 1926

June 26, 1926

August 14, 1926

August 26, 1926

October 2, 1926

December 4, 1926

January 8, 1927

February 19, 1927

March 12, 1927

April 16, 1927

June 4, 1927

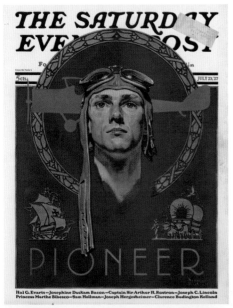

July 23, 1927

August 13, 1927

September 24, 1927

October 22, 1927

December 3, 1927

January 21, 1928

April 14, 1928

May 5, 1928

May 26, 1928

Benito Mussolini—Thomas McMorrow—Maximilian Foster—William Slavens McNutt
Peggy Wood—Clarence Budington Kelland—Fanny Heaslip Lea—Rear Admiral Magruder

June 23, 1928

Benito Mussolini—Rob Wagner—George Allan England—James Warner Bellah
Charles Francis Coe—F. Scott Fitzgerald—Maximilian Foster—Donald E. Keyhoe

July 21, 1928

E. W. Howe—Earl Derr Biggers—R. G. Kirk—George Weston—Will Payne
Don Marquis—Commander Ralph D. Weyerbacher—Leonard H. Nason

August 18, 1928

Isaac F. Marcosson—Booth Jameson
A. W. Somerville—William Hazlett Upson—Joseph Hergesheimer
Frederick Hazlitt Brennan—Leonard H. Nason—W. O. McGeehan

September 22, 1928

Merrie Christmas

December 8, 1928

Booth Tarkington—Corey Ford—Hugh Mac Nair Kahler—Edith Fitzgerald
Horatio Winslow—John Chapman Hilder—Will Payne—Ben Ames Williams

January 12, 1929

Garet Garrett—Mary F. Watkins—I. A. R. Wylie—Horatio Winslow—Kennett Harris
Ben Ames Williams—Clarence Budington Kelland—Rear Admiral T. P. Magruder

February 16, 1929

Samuel M. Vauclain—William Hazlett Upson—James Warner Bellah
Wesley Stout—Eleanor Mercein—Samuel Crowther—Booth Tarkington

March 9, 1929

E. Phillips Oppenheim—Nunnally Johnson—Wesley Stout—Almet Jenks
Struthers Burt—James Warner Bellah—Mary F. Watkins—Sam Hellman

April 20, 1929

May 4, 1929

June 15, 1929

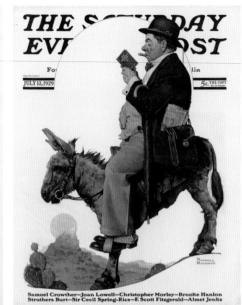

July 13, 1929

August 3, 1929

September 28, 1929

November 2, 1929

December 7, 1929

THE SATURDAY EVENING POST

THE DEPRESSION YEARS

(1930-1939)

With money scarce after the Stock Market Crash of 1929, the Thirties marked a decade of economic depression. Suffering through such trying times on a scale hitherto unknown, the public's knee-jerk reaction was to go to movies, amusement parks, and play cards and board games. Rockwell chose not to portray the all encompassing despair of suicides and poverty; rather he painted the quilt-like differences between Americans (*Stock Exchange Quotations*, January 18, 1930; page 180). In 1934, for the first time on a *Post* cover, he painted an African American boy chatting with a wealthy white woman who had fallen from her horse. The bare-footed child stands in contrast to her gleaming leather riding boots (*Woman in Riding Habit Fallen off Horse*, March 17, 1934; page 182). Soon, Rockwell's painting compositions expanded to fill the entire cover and sometimes extending beyond the edges, as in *Spring Tonic* (May 30, 1936; page 81). Often his images obstructed the *Post*'s well-known masthead with its thick, horizontal, double black lines. This technique offered the reader a bigger role in the scene and therefore it was more realistic. Rockwell's confidence continued to grow with his innovative images and he created scenes illustrating the contrast between 'haves' and 'have nots,' as in *Christmas-Knight Looking in Stained Glass Window* (December 6, 1930; page 71). Similarly, in *Volunteer Fireman* (March 28, 1931; page 75), the dichotomy between a fearless, yet naive youth is juxtaposed with a determined, measured professional. Such art works speak to Rockwell's ongoing development amidst a wave of introspection.

January 18, 1930

March 22, 1930

April 12, 1930

May 24, 1930

July 19, 1930

August 23, 1930

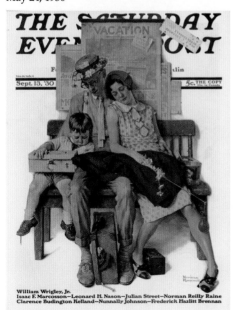

September 13, 1930

November 8, 1930

December 6, 1930

Clarence Budington Kelland—Mary Roberts Rinehart—Charles Brackett
E. Scott Fitzgerald—Edward Hungerford—Julian Street—Hugh Wiley

January 31, 1931

Myron C. Taylor—Alfred Noyes—Ida M. Evans—Clarence Budington Kelland
Isaac F. Marcosson—Struthers Burt—Bernard DeVoto—Ben Ames Williams

March 28, 1931

Eugene Manlove Rhodes—Robert Lansing—Arthur Train—Paul Jones
Guy Gilpatric—Leonard H. Nason—Kenneth Roberts—Sophie Kerr

April 18, 1931

Booth Tarkington—Horatio Winslow—Brooke Hanlon—Cora Harris
Norman Reilly Raine—James Warner Bellah—Ben Ames Williams

June 13, 1931

Jack Dempsey (Seconded by Charles Francis Coe)—Julian Street—Leonard H. Nason
Senator George H. Moses—Everett Rhodes Castle—E. R. Vadeboncoeur

July 25, 1931

Wythe Williams—Lucy Stone Terrill—William Beebe—F. Scott Fitzgerald
Jesse Rainsford Sprague—Leonard H. Nason—Dr. A. S. W. Rosenbach

September 5, 1931

Elizabeth Alexander—Edwin Lefèvre—J. P. Marquand—Samuel Crowther
Margaret Weymouth Jackson—Vincent Sheean—Paul Jones—Fannie Hurst

November 7, 1931

Merry Christmas

December 12, 1931

Stewart Edward White—George Wharton Pepper—Guglielmo Ferrero
Leonard H. Nason—San. Hellman—Brenda Ueland—Guy Gilpatric

January 30, 1932

★ 181

October 22, 1932

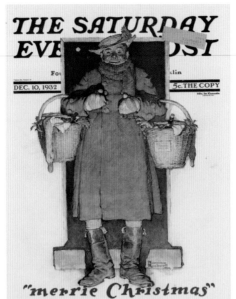

December 10, 1932

April 8, 1933

June 17, 1933

August 5, 1933

October 21, 1933

November 25, 1933

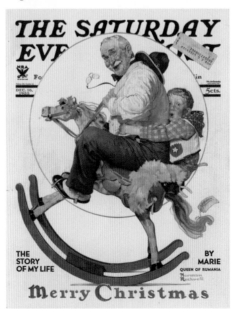

December 16, 1933

March 17, 1934

BOOTH TARKINGTON · COREY FORD · JOHN T. FOOTE

April 21, 1934

GARET GARRETT · ALICE DUER MILLER · WALTER EDMONDS

May 19, 1934

IN THIS NUMBER
GENERAL HUGH S. JOHNSON

June 30, 1934

BEGINNING
IN THIS ISSUE
PITCAIRN'S
ISLAND

By JAMES NORMAN HALL and CHARLES NORDHOFF

September 22, 1934

MAURICE WALSH · BOOTH TARKINGTON · RED GRANGE

October 20, 1934

December 15, 1934

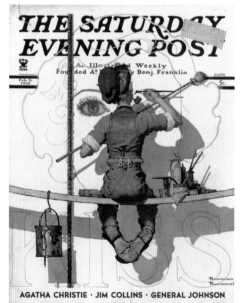

AGATHA CHRISTIE · JIM COLLINS · GENERAL JOHNSON

February 9, 1935

MANUEL KOMROFF · GILBERT SELDES · J. ROY STOCKTON

March 9, 1935

JOHN TAINTOR FOOTE · GUY GILPATRIC · JOSEPH HERGESHEIMER

April 27, 1935

★ 183

July 13, 1935

September 14, 1935

November 16, 1935

December 21, 1935

January 25, 1936

March 7, 1936

April 25, 1936

May 30, 1936

July 11, 1936

'OLLYWOOD ON THE THAMES—BY HENRY F. PRINGLE

September 26, 1936

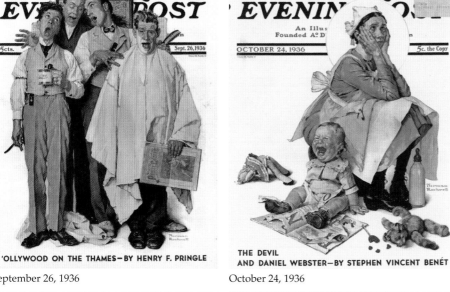

THE DEVIL
AND DANIEL WEBSTER—BY STEPHEN VINCENT BENÉT

October 24, 1936

FOOTBALL
WIFE
BY VIRGINIA BLACK

LIFER—BY CHARLES FRANCIS COE

November 21, 1936

SWING BUSINESS · HENRY ANTON STEIG

TISH GOES TO JAIL · MARY ROBERTS RINEHART

December 19, 1936

BEGINNING PADEREWSKI'S LIFE STORY

January 23, 1937

THE $47,000,000,000 BLIGHT—By SENATOR VANDENBERG

April 24, 1937

JESSE H. JONES · MARY ROBERTS RINEHART

June 12, 1937

WHITE-HOUSE TOMMY—By ALVA JOHNSTON

July 31, 1937

Beginning AND ONE WAS BEAUTIFUL By ALICE DUER MILLER

October 2, 1937

December 25, 1937

February 19, 1938

April 23, 1938

June 4, 1938

October 8, 1938

November 19, 1938

December 17, 1938

February 11, 1939

March 18, 1939

April 29, 1939

July 8, 1939

August 5, 1939

September 2, 1939

November 4, 1939

December 16, 1939

THE SATURDAY EVENING POST

WORLD WAR II AND AFTER
(1940-1949)

*W*ith the onset of World War II, Rockwell portrayed the home front with flirts, soda jerks, and 'Willie Gillis,' a favorite wartime character (pages 88-91). While other illustrators painted the battlefront, Rockwell posed Vermont neighbor Robert Buck, a short and unlikely warrior, as 'Wee Willie Gillis." For the March 1, 1941 issue, Rockwell boldly dropped one of the two black horizontal lines set below the *Post* masthead. Then on the remaining single white line, he proudly wrote that the magazine had reached a circulation of 3.3 million households – the largest magazine circulation in history. After May 30, 1942, the cover format changed further under Ben Hibbs, new *Post* Editor, allowing the artist-illustrators more artistic freedom and challenged them to "go further." When Rockwell painted the triumphant *Rosie the Riveter* (May 29, 1943, see opposite page), it became a perpetual iconic image for women's rights. His sequel to 'Rosie' three months later was *Miss Liberty* (September 4, 1943; page 101), a woman carrying the symbols of various men's jobs which were previously unattainable. Rockwell's cover *Disabled Veteran* (July 1, 1944; page 111) was a portrait of his Arlington, Vermont, neighbor Roy Cole as a wounded soldier. Rockwell produced the very popular *Bridge Game – The Bid* (May 15, 1948; page 125), featuring a simultaneous view of players' cards in a revolutionary one-point perspective taken from above. His April Fools covers have imbedded jokes abounding which automatically challenge viewers to decipher them. *Post* readers were most stymied by *April Fools – Girl with Shopkeeper* (April 3, 1948; page 119), with over sixty such jokes.

Opposite Page: Rosie the Riveter, 1943, oil on canvas.
An icon for the women's liberation movement and an enduring symbol of patriotism. It is the sister image to *Miss Liberty* (p. 101).

March 30, 1940

April 27, 1940

May 18, 1940

July 13, 1940

August 24, 1940

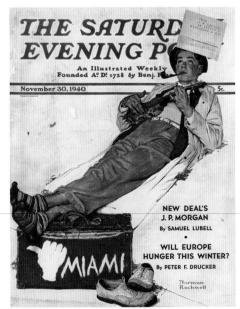

November 30, 1940

December 28, 1940

March 1, 1941

May 3, 1941

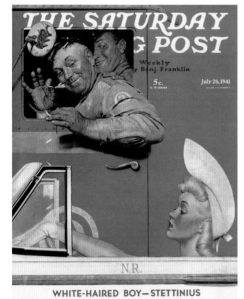

July 26, 1941

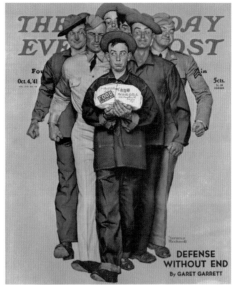

October 4, 1941

November 29, 1941

December 20, 1941

February 7, 1942

March 21, 1942

April 11, 1942

June 27, 1942

July 25, 1942

September 5, 1942

November 28, 1942

December 26, 1942

April 3, 1943

May 29, 1943

June 26, 1943

September 4, 1943

November 27, 1943

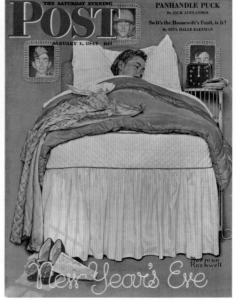

January 1, 1944

March 4, 1944

April 29, 1944

May 27, 1944

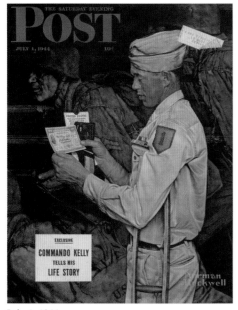

July 1, 1944

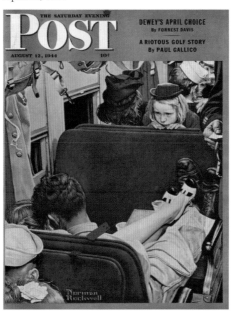

August 12, 1944

September 16, 1944

November 4, 1944

December 23, 1944

March 17, 1945

March 31, 1945

May 26, 1945

August 11, 1945

September 15, 1945

October 13, 1945

November 3, 1945

November 24, 1945

December 15, 1945

December 29, 1945

March 2, 1946

April 6, 1946

July 6, 1946

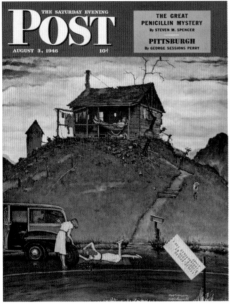

August 3, 1946

October 5, 1946

November 16, 1946

December 7, 1946

January 11, 1947

March 22, 1947

May 3, 1947

August 16, 1947

August 30, 1947

November 8, 1947

December 27, 1947

January 24, 1948

March 6, 1948

April 3, 1948

May 15, 1948

September 4, 1948

October 30, 1948

December 25, 1948

March 19, 1949

April 23, 1949

July 9, 1949

September 24, 1949

November 5, 1949

THE SATURDAY EVENING POST

THE FABULOUS FIFTIES

(1950-1959)

*W*orld War II's end brought the 'baby boom' and Levitt & Sons' Levittowns (rows of identical, inexpensive houses in the suburbs of New York City) were created to cater to returning veterans. Marilyn Monroe and James Dean were the Hollywood darlings, a polio vaccine was developed, Rosa Parks stood for African-American equality, and chrome muscle cars abounded. A rapacious consumer society fed on TV dinners and television advertising while billboards spoiled the countryside. The public turned increasingly to *Post* covers for guidance and to reflect upon their particular way of life as an affirmation of right versus wrong. As the *Post*'s premier cover artist and the recognized visionary of our national identity, Norman Rockwell was always the perfect choice to depict America. With a redesigned and modernized *Post* cover logo, he continued to paint images reflecting everyday life like *Shuffleton's Barbershop* (April 29, 1950; page 129), the traveling salesman in *Solitaire* (August 19, 1950; page 131), and *Boy Graduate* (June 6, 1959; page 141). The artist's son Tom modeled as the graduating student pictured against a background of newspaper headlines. The headlines were frightening as they contrasted worldwide problems with an optimistic, bewildered graduate. Norman Rockwell was not just the most beloved illustrator, but his name became a household word, synonymous with apple pie and baseball. He was now more than an illustrator, he was an institution, a legend in his own time.

Opposite Page: Portrait of Rockwell with *The Toss*, October 21, 1950

April 29, 1950

August 19, 1950

October 21, 1950

November 18, 1950

June 2, 1951

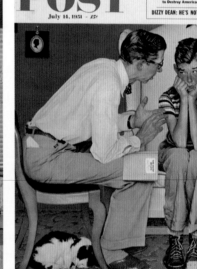

July 14, 1951

November 24, 1951

February 16, 1952

March 29, 1952

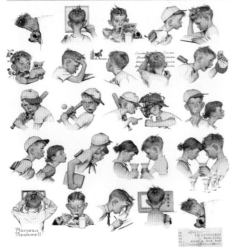

May 24, 1952

August 30, 1952

October 11, 1952

January 3, 1953

April 4, 1953

May 23, 1953

August 22, 1953

January 9, 1954

February 13, 1954

March 6, 1954

April 17, 1954

August 21, 1954

September 25, 1954

March 12, 1955

April 16, 1955

June 11, 1955

August 20, 1955

March 17, 1956

May 19, 1956

October 6, 1956

October 13, 1956

December 29, 1956

March 2, 1957

May 25, 1957

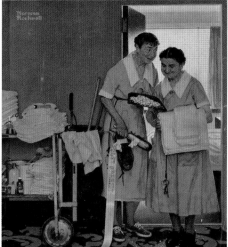

June 29, 1957

September 7, 1957

November 30, 1957

March 15, 1958

June 28, 1958

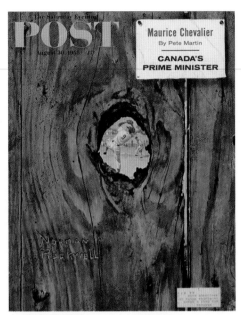

August 30, 1958

September 20, 1958

November 8, 1958

February 14, 1959

May 16, 1959

June 6, 1959

October 24, 1959

THE SATURDAY EVENING POST

AMERICAN HISTORY ILLUSTRATED
(1960-1963)

*D*uring the 1960s, political issues increasingly became Norman Rockwell's focus. The so-called "fine art world" struggled with cultural issues while representational art was virtually forbidden, and artists explored new movements such as Op Art, Pop Art and Assemblage. Society transformed and raised its collective fist in protest while students questioned authority. How could Norman Rockwell survive such a period? He did so by evolving with covers like his *Triple Self-Portrait* (February 13, 1960; page143). Rockwell created something entirely new, a self-portrait that cleverly showed his image three times. It was painted to herald the publication of his autobiography, which was serialized in the *Post*. Another breakthrough image, contemptuous of modern art (although Rockwell was enamored with Picasso), is entitled *The Connoisseur* (January 13, 1962; page 207). It shows a gentleman contemplating a Jackson Pollock-like Abstract Expressionist work in a museum setting. It was a direct stab at those promoting modern forms of art. He made his point by proving it was so easily copied by the *Post* illustrator himself. But, Rockwell tired of his work at the *Post*. He grew unhappy with the magazine's direction and the editors increasingly asking him to undertake portraits of celebrities and politicians. In 1963, Rockwell terminated his long-standing relationship and moved to *Look* magazine, bringing along his newfound interest in global issues. Perhaps the influence of American youth, or his children, caused this enlightenment. Rockwell's artworks thereafter provoked others to think more seriously for his audience had matured; America craved more than just entertainment. True to form, Norman Rockwell always gave his audience what they wanted, "*the Most American of American Art*,"™ our history illustrated.

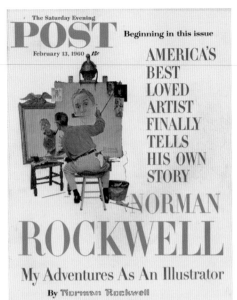

February 13, 1960

April 16, 1960

August 27, 1960

September 17, 1960

October 29, 1960

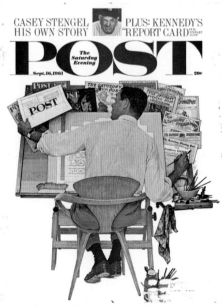

November 5, 1960

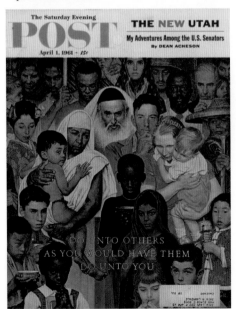

April 1, 1961

September 16, 1961

November 25, 1961

January 13, 1962

November 3, 1962

January 19, 1963

March 2, 1963

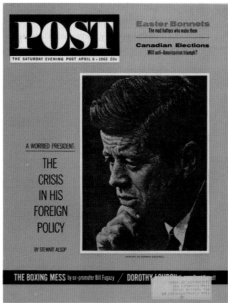

April 6, 1963

May 25, 1963

December 14, 1963

Above:
Oil studies of April 6, 1963 John F. Kennedy portraits, oil on board, 12" x 22", signed with Rockwell's comments to the art editor

Norman Rockwell in his studio, Stockbridge, MA, 1960.
Hanging on the wall is an original oil by Howard Pyle (center) and reproductions of works by Rembrandt, Bruegel, Vermeer, Michelangelo and Canaletto with some of Rockwell's studies on the ledge.

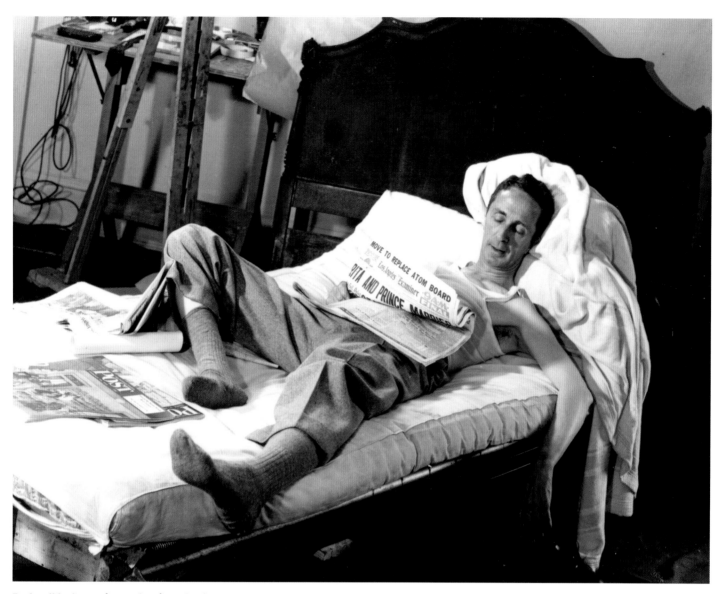

Rockwell looking exhausted with a pile of *Post* magazines and newspapers, circa May 30, 1949
Possible unused idea for *Travelling Salesman Saturday Evening Post* cover.
Photograph: Pete Todd, Los Angeles County Art Institute

FINIS

ACKNOWLEDGEMENTS

We are sincerely indebted to those persons and institutions who assisted in creating this ground-breaking exhibition and accompanying catalogue.

The staffs at the *National Museum of American Illustration*, Newport, RI; *American Illustrators Gallery*, New York City; and *Dulwich Picture Gallery*, London, England receive our gratitude and plaudits for their hard-working and dedicated efforts.

We would like to mention, at the *National Museum of American Illustration* (NMAI), Eric Brocklehurst, Jill Perkins and Catherine Smith, and at the *American Illustrators Gallery* (AIG), Andrew Goffman and Drew Wingert. We particularly wish to acknowledge Sara Bliss (NMAI) and Christine Shannon (AIG), for their labors over the requisite editing, publishing, organization and production efforts.

We give thanks to *Dulwich Picture Gallery* (DPG) team, Iain Betterton, Lily Harriss, Ellie Manwell, Mella Shaw, Lizzie Watson, and lastly their tireless leader, Ian Dejardin. Ian's clear and serious love of American illustration art was apparent from the moment we met. His enthusiastic embracing of the acorn of a thought to undertake a Rockwell exhibition has driven this entire process. We thank Ian for his humour, perseverance and professionalism.

At the *Norman Rockwell Museum* at Stockbridge (NRM), we would like to thank Laurie Norton Moffatt and Stephanie Plunkett, who have always supported our scholarly efforts at the NMAI, and to Corry Kanzenberg, who assisted us with photographic materials. Thanks to Maureen Hennesey and Linda Szekely Pero, both formerly of the NRM, who assisted us with research and editorial comments over the years. For their efforts, and all of the above mentioned individuals, we are most grateful.

We could not have undertaken this ambitious catalogue without the generous support of an Anonymous Benefactor and we offer many thanks for her continuing support.

Finally, we acknowledge those collectors who graciously loaned their paintings to the exhibition. Their generosity in sharing these art treasures with the public is admirable and greatly appreciated by everyone.

Judy Goffman Cutler, Museum Director
Laurence S. Cutler, Chairman/CEO
National Museum of American Illustration
Vernon Court
Newport, Rhode Island

Winter 2010

Opposite: Norman Rockwell's *Triple Self-Portrait*, 1960, oil on canvas, 44 1/2" x 34 3/4", Norman Rockwell Musem, Stockbridge, MA (Upper right tacked to Rockwell's canvas are self portraits by Durer, Rembrandt, Picasso, and Van Gogh)

SELECT BIBLIOGRAPHY

This bibliography is an assist to those undertaking further research on Norman Rockwell. It is not comprehensive, but rather a starting point to delve further into those forces which helped to create this extraordinary individual. Hopefully, this exhibition and catalogue will ignite further interest and research.

Bauer, Fred. *The Faith of America*. New York: Guideposts, 1980.

Bradley, Will. "The Art of Illustration." *The Nation* July, 1913.

Brooklyn Museum. *A Century of American Illustration*. Intro. by Duncan F. Cameron. New York: Brooklyn Museum Press, 1972.

Buechner, Thomas S. *Norman Rockwell, Artist and Illustrator*. New York: Harry N. Abrams, 1970.

Buechner, Thomas S. *Norman Rockwell: A Sixty Year Retrospective*. New York: Harry N. Abrams, 1972.

Buechner, Thomas S. *Norman Rockwell's America*. Daytona Beach, FL: Museum of Arts and Sciences, 1976.

Buechner, Thomas S. *The Norman Rockwell Treasury*. New York: Harry N. Abrams, Inc., 1979.

Butterfield, Roger. *The Saturday Evening Post Treasury*. New York: Simon & Schuster Inc., 1954.

Claridge, Laura. *Norman Rockwell, A Life*. New York: Random House, 2001.

Cohn, Jan. *Covers of the Saturday Evening Post*. New York: Viking Studio Books, 1995.

Csatari, Joseph. *Norman Rockwell's Boy Scouts of America*. New York: DK Publishing, 2009.

Cutler, Laurence S., and Goffman, Judy. *Norman Rockwell*. Tokyo, Japan: Brain Trust, 1992.

Cutler, Laurence S., and Judy Goffman. *The Great American Illustrators*. Tokyo: The Great American Illustrators Catalogue Committee, 1993.

Cutler, Laurence S., and Judy Goffman Cutler. *J.C. Leyendecker: American Imagist*. New York: Harry N. Abrams, 2008.

Cutler, Laurence S. and Judy Goffman. *Maxfield Parrish*. London: Bison Books Ltd.; Greenwich, CT: Brompton Books, 1993.

Cutler, Laurence S. and Judy Goffman Cutler and the National Museum of American Illustration. *Maxfield Parrish and the American Imagists*. Edison, NJ: The Wellfleet Press, 2004.

Cutler, Laurence S. and Judy A. G. Cutler, *Maxfield Parrish: A Retrospective*. Tokyo: A Retrospective Catalogue Committee, Tokyo, 1995.

Cutler, Laurence S., and Judy A. G. Cutler. *Maxfield Parrish: A Retrospective*. San Francisco: Pomegranate Artbooks, 1995.

Cutler, Laurence S., and Judy A. G. Cutler with The National Museum of American Illustration. *Maxfield Parrish: Treasures of Art*. New York: Gramercy Books/Random House Value Publishing, Inc., 1999.

Cutler, Laurence S., and Judy Cutler and the National Museum of American Illustration. *Norman Rockwell and his Mentor, JC Leyendecker*. Newport, RI: National Museum of American Illustration, 2010.

Elzea, Rowland. *The Golden Age of Illustration, 1880 - 1914*. Wilmington, DE: Delaware Art Museum, 1972.

Folds, David P. Jr. *The Norman Rockwell Treasury 1979*. Boynton Beach, Florida: Futura Printing, Inc., 1978.

Goffman, Judy, Davide Faccioli and Manuela Teatini, eds. *Norman Rockwell*. Milan, Italy: Electa Publishing, 1990.

Goffman, Judy. *Norman Rockwell: An American Tradition*. Greenville, South Carolina: Greenville Museum of Art, 1986.

Goffman, Judy. *Norman Rockwell: The Great American Storyteller*. Jackson, Mississippi: Mississippi Museum of Art, 1988-89.

Grunwald Center for the Graphic Arts. *The American Personality: The Artist-Illustrator of Life in the United States, 1860-1930*. Intro. by E. Maurice Bloch. Los Angeles: University of California, 1976.

Guptill, Arthur L. *Norman Rockwell, Illustrator*. New York: Watson-Guptill, 1946.

Hambidge, Jay. *Dynamic Symmetry of The Greek Vase*. New Haven: Yale University Press, 1920.

Hambidge, Jay. *The Elements of Dynamic Symmetry*. New York: Brentanos, 1926.

Hennessey, Maureen Hart and Anne Knutson. *Norman Rockwell: Pictures for the American People*. Atlanta, Georgia: High Museum of Art; Stockbridge, Massachusetts: The Norman Rockwell Museum; New York: Harry Abrams, Inc., 2000.

Marling, Karal Ann. *Norman Rockwell*. New York: Harry N. Abrams in association with the National Museum of American Art, Smithsonian Institution, 1997.

Mecklenburg, Virgina M. *Telling Stories, Norman Rockwell from the collections of George Lucas and Steven Spielberg*. New York: Abrams, 2010.

Mendoza, George. *Norman Rockwell's Boys and Girls at Play*. New York: Harry N. Abrams, Inc., 1976.

Meyer, Susan E. *America's Great Illustrators*. New York: Harry N. Abrams, Inc., 1978.

Meyer, Susan E. *Norman Rockwell's People*. New York: Harry N. Abrams, Inc., 1981.

Moffatt, Laurie Norton. *Norman Rockwell-A Definitive Catalogue: Volumes 1 & 2*. Stockbridge, Massachusetts: The Norman Rockwell Museum, 1986.

Montgomery, Elizabeth Miles. *Norman Rockwell*. North Dighton, MA: World Publications Group, Inc., 1989.

Norman Rockwell Album, The. Intro. by S. Lane Faison, Jr. Garden City, New York: Doubleday & Company, Inc., 1961.

Pero, Linda Szekely. *American Chronicles: The Art of Norman Rockwell*. Stockbridge, MA: The Norman Rockwell Museum, 2007.

Pitz, Henry Clarence. *The Practice of Illustration*. New York: Watson-Guptill, 1947.

Pitz, Henry Clarence. *200 Years of American Illustration*. New York: Society of Illustrators, 1977.

Rivoli, Kevin and Norman Rockwell. *In Search of Norman Rockwell's America*. New York: Howard Books, 2008.

Rockwell, Norman. *Rockwell on Rockwell, How I Make a Picture*. New York: Watson-Guptill, 1979.

Rockwell, Norman, and Thomas Rockwell. *Norman Rockwell: My Adventures as an Illustrator*. Garden City, New York: Doubleday & Company, Inc., 1960.

Rockwell, Norman, and Thomas Rockwell. *Norman Rockwell, My Adventures as an Illustrator*. New York: Abrams, 1988.

Rockwell, Tom. *The Best of Norman Rockwell: A Celebration of America's Favorite Illustrator*. Philadelphia: Courage Books, 1988.

Schau, Michael. "All-American Girl." *The Art of Coles Phillips*. New York: Watson-Guptill, 1975.

Schick, Ron. *Norman Rockwell: Behind the Camera*. New York: Little, Brown and Company, 2009.

Sommer, Robin Langley. *Norman Rockwell*. North Dighton, MA: World Publications Group, Inc., 2006.

Stoltz, Donald R., and Marshall L. Stoltz. *The Advertising World of Norman Rockwell*. New York: Harrison House, 1986.

Stoltz, Donald R., and Marshall L. Stoltz. *Norman Rockwell and the Saturday Evening Post: Vols. 1, 2 & 3*. New York: MJF Books, 1994.

Wagner, Margaret E. *Maxfield Parrish & the Illustrators of the Golden Age*. Rohnert Park, California: Pomegranate Communications, Inc., 2000.

Watson, Ernest W. *Forty Illustrators and How They Work*. New York: Watson-Guptill, 1946.

ILLUSTRATION LIST*

*All artworks listed are by Norman Rockwell unless otherwise noted

Opposite: Detail from Norman Rockwell's Santa's Workshop (page 57)

NATIONAL MUSEUM OF AMERICAN ILLUSTRATION
MISSION STATEMENT

The National Museum of American Illustration (NMAI) is an independent, educational, and aesthetic nonprofit organization with the goal to educate and enlighten the global public about American Illustration art in a Gilded Age mansion.

The National Museum of American Illustration was founded in 1998 by Judy Goffman Cutler and Laurence S. Cutler, to house their art collection primarily from the 'Golden Age of American Illustration.' Yet, the museum exhibits American illustration from all periods. The Museum venue is Vernon Court (1898), an interpretation of an 18th century French chateau from the 'Gilded Age of Architecture,' designed by Carrére & Hastings, architects for many notable buildings such as the NY Public Library, the US Senate and House Office Buildings, Lord Duveen's New York Galleries, the Neue Gallery, The Flagler Museum, and Frick Collection. The three acre grounds were inspired by Henry VIII's gardens created for his ill-fated Queen, Anne Boleyn at Hampton Court Palace. The adjacent three acres known as Stonearce were designed by the first American landscape architect, Frederick Law Olmsted. This property has been restored and revitalized into the Frederick Law Olmsted Park.

The National Museum of American Illustration (NMAI), is administered by the American Civilization Foundation, an IRS approved 501 c3 nonprofit organization. The NMAI is an independent, educational, and aesthetic organization with the mission to share illustration masterpieces with the public worldwide.

The NMAI is not a federal government organization nor is it federally funded, it exists due to the benevolence of our founders and with further support from people like you.

The NMAI was founded in 1998 and opened to the public on July 4th, 2000. It is listed on the National Register of Historic Places and is considered a *national cultural treasure.*

The NMAI is a member of the *American Association of Museums, American Federation of the Arts, Museum Store Association, National Association for Olmsted Parks, New England Association of Museums, Newport County Chamber of Commerce,* and *Attractions Council of Newport County.*

Opposite: Norman Rockwell posing with *Samson Tearing Down the Temple* (Actor Victor Mature as 'Samson') 1949